Gar-Field Hi
14000 Smoketown Road
Woodbridge, VA 22192

MW01118702

BULGARIA
in Pictures

VGS

Margaret J. Goldstein

Lerner Publications Company

Contents

Website address: www.lernerbooks.com

Lerner Publications Company
A division of Lerner Publishing Group
241 First Avenue North
Minneapolis, MN 55401 U.S.A.

web enhanced @ www.vgsbooks.com

CULTURAL LIFE 48

► Music and Dance. Language and Literature.
Modern Media. Religion. Holidays and Festivals.
Food. Sports and Recreation.

THE ECONOMY 58

► Services. Industry. Agriculture. Transportation.
The Future.

FOR MORE INFORMATION

T 49371

Library of Congress Cataloging-in-Publication Data

Goldstein, Margaret J.
    Bulgaria in pictures / by Margaret J. Goldstein.—Rev. and expanded.
      p. cm. — [Visual geography series]
    Includes bibliographical references and index.
    ISBN: 0-8225-3057-0 (lib. bdg. : alk. paper)
    1. Bulgaria—Juvenile literature. I. Title. II. Series: Visual geography series (Minneapolis, Minn.)
DR67.7.G65 2005
949.9—dc22   2004021745

Manufactured in the United States of America
1 2 3 4 5 6 - BP - 10 09 08 07 06 05

INTRODUCTION

Bulgaria, a country of roughly 7.5 million people, lies on the Balkan Peninsula (also called the Balkans) of southeastern Europe. Bulgaria's history dates back thousands of years. Among its earliest inhabitants were the Thracians, an ancient civilization. The Thracians had a rich culture, with a strong tradition of poetry and music. Thracian ruins can still be seen in modern Bulgaria.

A number of outside groups arrived in Bulgaria in ancient times. First the Macedonians and later the Romans conquered the region. In the fifth and seventh centuries A.D., Slavs and Bulgars controlled Bulgaria. Afterward, the Bulgarian Empire became the most powerful state in the Balkans. Its craftspeople created splendid churches and impressive artworks.

In the late fourteenth century, the Ottoman (Turkish) Empire conquered the Balkans. Bulgarians lived under Turkish domination until the 1800s, when the Ottoman Empire weakened. Aided by Russia, Bulgaria gained partial independence in 1878 and full independence in 1908.

During the early 1900s, Bulgaria struggled to maintain a stable government. After World War II (1939–1945), the Communist Party seized power in Bulgaria. The Communists controlled agriculture and industry and banned opposing political parties. Along with several other Eastern European nations, Bulgaria was part of the Soviet bloc—countries closely allied with the Communist Soviet Union. The Communist era was a bleak one for Bulgaria. The government strictly controlled art, writing, and other creative pursuits. People were not free to operate their own businesses or voice their political opinions. Around 1990 Bulgarians ended their Communist regime and established a new, democratic republic.

With the fall of Communism, Bulgaria flourished. In the early 2000s, it has a rich music scene, numerous publishing houses, and fascinating art and history museums. Bulgarians celebrate their centuries-old traditions at numerous folk festivals every year. Many tourists come to Bulgaria to enjoy its picturesque mountains, quaint villages, seaside resorts, and ancient ruins.

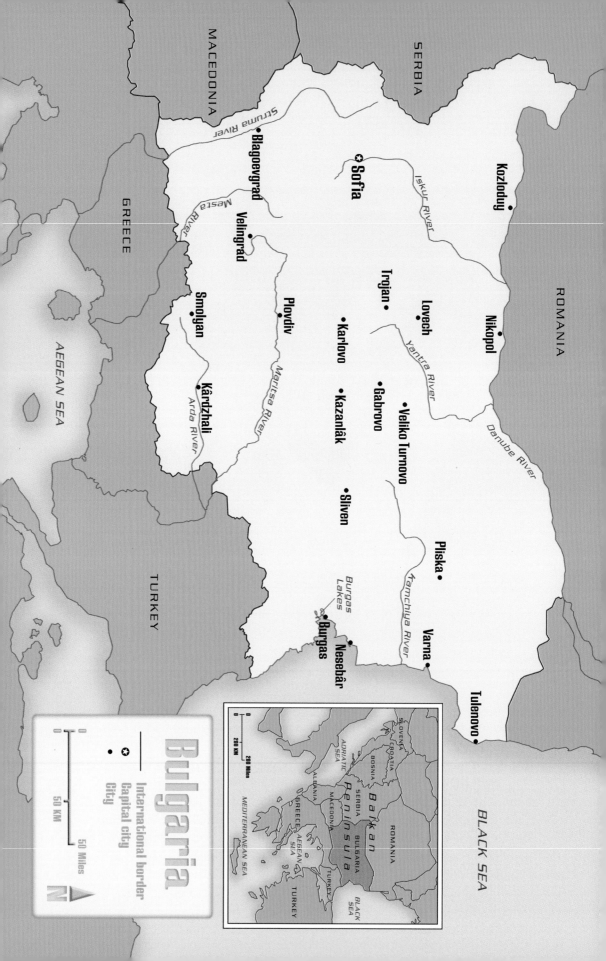

Modern Bulgaria faces many challenges, though, most notably a struggling economy. Many Bulgarians are poor, and Bulgarian industries are not strong. However, the Bulgarian government has taken many steps to improve the economy. Bulgaria plans to join the European Union, an alliance of European nations that cooperate in business and politics. Best of all, Bulgarians are enjoying living in a free, democratic society. As the Communist era fades from memory, Bulgarians are looking to the future with great optimism.

THE LAND

Bulgaria is in a mountainous region of southeastern Europe. Turkey and Greece lie south of Bulgaria. The republics of Macedonia and Serbia are Bulgaria's western neighbors. Romania sits to the north. The Danube River runs along the Bulgarian-Romanian border. Eastern Bulgaria has a 175-mile (281-kilometer) coastline on the Black Sea.

Bulgaria's total land area is 42,823 square miles (110,911 sq. km), about the size of Tennessee. The greatest distance from north to south is 170 miles (273 km). East to west, Bulgaria stretches 306 miles (492 km) at its widest point.

Geographical Regions

Bulgaria has four main geographical regions: the Danubian Plain, the Balkan Mountains, the Sredna Gora and lowlands (Thracian Plain and Burgas Lowland), and the Rhodope Mountains. The Danubian Plain covers the northern part of the country, between the Danube River and

the Balkan Mountains. This plateau is an area of fertile, rolling farm-land, with several rivers running north into the Danube.

In the southern part of the plateau, the land gradually slopes upward to meet the Balkan Mountains. This range runs across the country from east to west. It reaches its highest point in the near cen-ter of the country at Botev Peak, 7,795 feet (2,376 meters) above sea level. Nearby is Shipka Pass, the site of a famous nineteenth-century battle against the Turks. Sofia, the Bulgarian capital, is located just southwest of the mountains.

South of the Balkan Mountains is the Sredna Gora, which means "middle forest." This wooded ridge is about 100 miles (161 km) long and climbs to 5,000 feet (1,524 m) high. Between the Balkan Mountains and the Sredna Gora lies the narrow Valley of the Roses, where farm-ers grow roses for their fragrant oil, which is used to make perfume. The southern slopes of the Sredna Gora descend to the Thracian Plain, a region of hills and lowlands stretching along the Maritsa River valley.

The flat Burgas Lowland, an extension of the Thracian Plain, reaches east to the Black Sea coast.

The Rhodope Mountains dominate southwestern Bulgaria. This range features rocky peaks, steep gorges, and a few freshwater lakes. The range includes the rugged Rila Mountains south of Sofia and the Pirin Mountains, which run to Bulgaria's border with Greece. The highest point in Bulgaria, Musala Peak, is in the Rila Mountains. This peak measures 9,597 feet (2,925 m) above sea level.

Because Bulgaria is mountainous, it is full of fascinating caves and rock formations. Many of the sites have colorful names, such as the Miraculous Bridges (a series of natural stone bridges over a river) and the Devil's Throat (a vast, spooky cave).

Rivers, Lakes, and the Sea

Bulgaria has many small, fast-moving streams and rivers that flow from highland areas down to the valleys and lowlands. Throughout the centuries, Bulgarians have pumped water from these rivers, especially the Danube, for irrigation (watering crops). Bulgarians have also dammed rivers to create hydroelectric power (electricity generated by rushing water) stations and reservoirs (human-made lakes) that provide water for farms and cities. The nation also has several natural lakes, including the Burgas Lakes surrounding the city of Burgas.

A dam on the Arda River in southern Bulgaria provides hydroelectricity to neighboring areas.

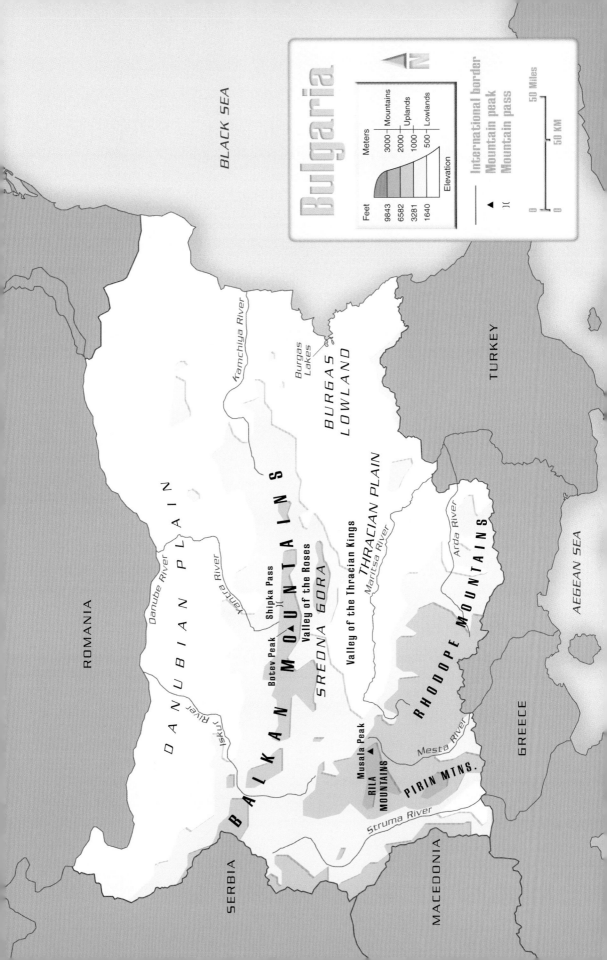

Bulgaria

Elevation

Feet	Meters	
9843	3000	Mountains
6582	2000	Uplands
3281	1000	
1640	500	Lowlands

International border

▲ Mountain peak

)(Mountain pass

0   50 Miles

0   50 KM

ROMANIA

BLACK SEA

SERBIA

DANUBIAN PLAIN

Danube River

Iskur River

Ogosta River

Yantra River

Kamchiya River

BALKAN MOUNTAINS

Botev Peak ▲

Shipka Pass)(

Valley of the Roses

SREDNA GORA

Valley of the Thracian Kings

THRACIAN PLAIN

Maritsa River

BURGAS LOWLAND

Burgas Lakes

RILA MOUNTAINS

Musala Peak ▲

Mesta River

PIRIN MTNS.

RHODOPE MOUNTAINS

Arda River

Struma River

MACEDONIA

GREECE

TURKEY

AEGEAN SEA

The Danube River is the second-longest river in Europe, flowing through nine countries on its way to the Black Sea. In some spots, the river is 1 mile (1.6 km) wide. In Bulgaria the Danube forms most of the nation's northern border with Romania. It is the country's only navigable (large enough for ships) waterway. Cargo ships carrying grain, coal, and industrial goods travel the river regularly. In Bulgaria as well as other nations, the Danube is heavily polluted by industrial waste.

The largest tributary (feeder river) of the Danube is the Iskur, which rises in the Rila Mountains, cuts through the Balkan range, then flows northeastward through the Danubian Plain. The Kamchiya River, in the eastern Balkan Mountains, reaches the Black Sea south of the port of Varna.

The source of the Maritsa River, the main waterway of the Thracian Plain, lies high in the Rila Mountains. Cities, villages, and farms dot the broad Maritsa River valley. After leaving Bulgaria, the Maritsa forms the border between Greece and Turkey before emptying into the Aegean Sea. The Struma and Mesta rivers tumble down steep mountain gorges in southwestern Bulgaria and flow southward into Greece.

The Black Sea, Bulgaria's eastern border, is a large inland sea between Europe and Asia. As a crossroads between two continents, the sea has long played an important role in commerce and warfare. In Bulgaria the sea is the site of several port cities, including Burgas and Varna. Many seaside resorts sit along the coastline as well.

> Visit www.vgsbooks.com for links to websites with additional information about Bulgaria's waterways.

Climate

Bulgaria's climate varies, from north to south and from the mountain ranges to the lowlands. The Danubian Plain has hot summers and cold winters, with heavy winds from the north and east. Sofia, in a mountainous area, has a mild climate. Temperatures there average 29°F (−1.5°C) in January (the coldest month) and 70°F (21°C) in July (the warmest month).

Slightly warmer temperatures are common on the Thracian Plain, where the Balkan Mountains shelter cities and farms from cold northern winds. Temperatures in Plovdiv, the largest town on the Thracian Plain, average 32°F (0°C) in January and 75°F (24°C) in July. The Black Sea coast and the southern Rhodope Mountains have warmer, sunnier climates.

Overall, Bulgaria receives an average of 25 inches (64 centimeters) of precipitation (rain and snow) each year. This moisture falls mostly

Brown bears are protected in a wildlife reserve in the Rila Mountains near Sofia. Visit www.vgsbooks.com for links to more information about Bulgaria's wildlife.

as rain on the Bulgarian plains and lowlands and as snow in the highlands. A few mountain peaks are covered in snow most of the year. Most rain falls in late spring. Sometimes the nation suffers from drought in late summer.

Flora and Fauna

Bulgaria has extensive forestland. In fact, about 35 percent of the country is covered by forests. Species such as beech, oak, pines, and fir grow in the mountains. Walnut and chestnut trees are common in the Maritsa River valley. Woody vines, flowering trees, and other subtropical plants grow along the rivers of the Burgas Lowland and on the Black Sea coast. Lowland areas also have wild apple, pear, and plum trees.

Bulgaria is home to thousands of animal species. Mammals such as bears, wolves, elks, deer, boars, foxes, and wildcats live in the mountains. Bird species include quails, turtledoves, cormorants, pelicans, and owls. Sturgeon, whitefish, and carp swim in Bulgaria's rivers, and small numbers of seals and dolphins live off the Black Sea coast north of Varna.

Environmental Issues

Like most modern nations, Bulgaria suffers from a variety of environmental problems. Its factories and power plants release heavy amounts

An oil refinery outside Burgas releases thick smoke into the air.

of pollution into the air. Many of these facilities are old and do not have modern pollution-control devices. Some power plants produce nuclear energy, creating dangerous radioactive waste.

In addition to polluting the air, Bulgarian industries release pollution into rivers and the Black Sea. The Danube River, which begins in Germany, contains pollution from countries to the north of Bulgaria. Then Bulgaria adds more waste to the river. Bulgarian farmers use pesticides to kill insects and fertilizers to help their crops grow. Washed away by the rain, these chemicals eventually run off into rivers and the sea. Both air and water pollution are harmful to wildlife and to human health. For instance, pollution in the Black Sea has killed off many fish.

In Bulgaria's vast forests, logging companies cut trees for their valuable timber. As forests are cut, the plants and animals there have fewer places to live. The growth of big cities and the creation of new roads and businesses have also hurt wilderness areas and wildlife. Some animal species, such as certain kinds of otters and bats, have become endangered (likely to die out). Legal and illegal hunting has further hurt animal populations in Bulgaria. Large numbers of bears, for example, have been killed.

The Bulgarian government's Ministry of Environment and Water cleans up polluted areas and protects wilderness from new pollution. The ministry creates rules that businesses must follow to limit pollution. The Bulgarian government has also created twelve national parks and numerous other preserves throughout the country. These areas are off-limits to building, hunting, and other activities that can harm plants and animals. But visitors are welcome to hike through the parks and preserves and view the wildlife there. Some private groups also work to fight pollution and protect the environment in Bulgaria.

Natural Resources

Bulgaria's most valuable natural resource is the black, fertile soil of the northern Danubian Plain. The Thracian Plain and the Maritsa River valley also boast good soil. About 39 percent of Bulgaria's land is arable, or suitable for farming. Farmers grow apples, pears, potatoes, tomatoes, tobacco, wheat, barley, sunflowers, sugar beets, and other crops. Some farmers raise livestock. Others grow roses for their fragrant oil. Still others grow grapes for making wine. Bulgaria's forests are another valuable resource. Timber from the forests is used to make homes, office buildings, and household products.

Bulgaria has coal deposits in the Balkan Mountains. Oil reserves are found at Tulenovo near the Black Sea and in offshore wells near Varna. Dams on the Iskur, the Struma, and other rivers supply Bulgaria with hydroelectric power.

Bulgaria also has metal and mineral deposits. Iron ore is found near Sofia and along the Black Sea near Burgas. The Burgas Lowland has copper and manganese deposits. Gold is mined east of Sofia. Small amounts of lead, zinc, and copper are found in the Rhodope and Balkan mountains. Kaolin (a white clay used to make pottery), pyrite, bauxite, and sulfur are also mined in Bulgaria.

Bulgarian farmers grow **fields of wheat** and other crops.

◉ Cities

Bulgaria's population numbers more than 7.5 million people. Nearly 70 percent of the population lives in urban areas. The biggest cities are Sofia, Plovdiv, Varna, and Burgas.

SOFIA (population 1.2 million) is Bulgaria's capital. It sits in a high mountain basin in the western part of the country. The ancient Thracians settled in Sofia before 1000 B.C. They named their settlement Sardonopolis and later Serdica. The Romans captured the settlement in 29 B.C. Slavs arrived in the sixth and seventh centuries A.D., and Bulgars came in A.D. 809. Each new group gave the city a new name. In the fourteenth century, the name changed to Sofia, after the city's Church of Saint Sofia. In 1879, after liberation from the Ottoman Turks, Sofia became the capital of Bulgaria. The United States and its allies heavily bombed Sofia during World War II. After the war, the city was extensively rebuilt.

Modern Sofia is the country's cultural capital as well as the seat of government. It has universities, technical colleges, museums, and an opera house. Visitors to Sofia can see Roman-era ruins and mosques (Islamic houses of worship) from the Ottoman period. The fountains, shade trees, and pleasant lawns of the Sofia City Garden offer a place to rest in the city's crowded center.

Modern Sofia is also a transportation hub. From here, roads and railroads lead west to Serbia, north to the Danube Plateau, and east to the Thracian Plain. Sofia also has a major international airport. The city has a thriving industrial sector. Its factories produce textiles, chemicals, machinery, shoes, clothing, and transportation equipment.

PLOVDIV, the country's second largest city (population 375,000), is on the Maritsa River. Plovdiv traces its origins to the Thracians, who built a city called Eumolpias on this site as early as 5000 B.C. Macedonians conquered Eumolpias in 341 B.C. The city later became the capital of the Roman province of Thrace.

Modern Plovdiv has a number of cultural and historical offerings, including art museums, centuries-old churches and mosques, and a remarkable Roman amphitheater (outdoor theater). Visitors can also see the ruins of Eumolpias. The city is an important commercial center for southern Bulgaria, with a variety of food processing plants and factories.

VARNA (population 350,000) is a major port on the Black Sea. The Thracians were the city's first inhabitants. Then Greeks settled the

Cargo ships pull into the harbor at the **port city of Burgas.** Burgas is the largest port city in Bulgaria.

area, calling their settlement Odessos. In the following centuries, each conquering group—the Macedonians, the Romans, and the Ottoman Turks—left its stamp on the city. Modern Varna is a charming seaside town with a lively arts scene and great beaches. It also has factories, port facilities, and a naval base. Visitors can also see ruins and buildings from ancient times.

BURGAS (population 210,000) is another Black Sea port city. It has been home to Thracians, Greeks, Romans, and others in its long history. The modern town has fish canneries, an oil refinery, port facilities, and industry, along with a few attractions for tourists. The nearby Burgas Lakes form a large wetland (marshy and swampy area) that is home to a nature preserve and about 60 percent of the nation's bird species.

 Visit www.vgsbooks.com for links to websites with additional information about Bulgaria's cities.

HISTORY AND GOVERNMENT

Stone Age cave dwellers, the first inhabitants of modern-day Bulgaria, lived in the region about forty thousand years ago. Archaeologists have discovered prehistoric tools and weapons in several Bulgarian caves. Some early inhabitants painted pictures of humans and animals on cave walls. The first inhabitants were probably nomadic (traveling) hunter-gatherers. They moved from place to place, looking for edible plants and herds of animals for hunting. By about 5000 B.C., some people lived in permanent villages in small houses made of mud.

Over the centuries, different tribes (large family groups) in the region created a unified kingdom known as Thrace. The Thracians built towns, fortresses, and farms. They traded materials such as copper and gold with neighboring peoples. Gradually, the Thracians developed a complex culture, noted for its music and poetry. The Thracians worshiped many gods. They buried their dead in above-ground tombs called *mogili*. They were also accomplished warriors.

The Greeks were a powerful civilization based to the south of Thrace. Starting in the seventh century B.C., the Greeks established several settlements in Thracian territory, mainly on the Black Sea coast. The Greeks and the Thracians lived together peacefully. They exchanged items such as pottery and jewelry. Many Thracians learned to speak the Greek language and copied Greek artistic styles. In turn, the Greeks adopted some Thracian religious beliefs. For a time, Thracian rulers had a political alliance with Athens, a powerful Greek city.

In the fourth century B.C., Philip II, the ruler of Macedonia in northern Greece, attacked and defeated Thrace. After Philip's death, his son, Alexander the Great, led Macedonian armies through Thrace and Asia Minor (modern-day Turkey). Alexander then conquered much of the Middle East and Central Asia. Macedonian rule did not last long. Thrace regained its independence after Alexander's death in 323 B.C. and the collapse of his empire.

THRACIAN TOMBS

The Bulgarian countryside is full of Thracian tombs, some of them untouched for thousands of years and others excavated (unearthed and studied) and open to the public. The Valley of the Thracian Kings, northwest of the city of Kazanlâk, contains roughly 1,500 mogili. The most elaborate resting places for wealthy and powerful Thracians contain several rooms, domed roofs, and elaborate wall murals.

The region's valuable gold mines and prosperous seaports soon attracted another powerful group, the Romans. Based on the Italian Peninsula, the Romans set out to expand their empire in the 200s B.C. After defeating Macedonia in the 140s B.C., the Romans drove northward to the Danube River. By A.D. 46, the Romans controlled the entire Balkan Peninsula (as well as much of western Europe, North Africa, and the Middle East).

Rome split the Balkan Peninsula into two provinces (political divisions)—Moesia, between the Danube River and the Balkan Mountains; and Thrace, to the south. Roman soldiers and farmers settled in the two

Roman ruins in Plovdiv exist side by side with architecture from other eras.

provinces and built new roads, fortifications, and cities. As part of the vast Roman Empire, the provinces had to send soldiers to serve in the Roman army. The provinces also shipped grain and other resources to the capital city of Rome.

Roman control weakened in the third century, when the Goths, a war-like tribe from northern Europe, began to attack cities and farms on the Balkan Peninsula. Further weakened, the Roman Empire split into eastern and western halves in the late fourth century. The Balkan Peninsula became part of the Eastern Roman Empire (or the Byzantine Empire), with its capital at Constantinople (modern-day Istanbul, Turkey).

The Bulgarian Kingdom

In the fifth century, the Byzantine Empire declined. Foreign groups invaded the empire in many places. On the Balkan Peninsula, Slavs arrived from the plains north of the Black Sea (modern-day Poland and Ukraine), followed about a century later by Bulgars from Central Asia. Byzantine forces were too weak to defend the peninsula from the invaders.

The Bulgars, the stronger of the two newcomers, quickly took control of the region, subduing the Slavs and the remaining Thracians. Although the Bulgars were more powerful, the Slavs were more numerous. So the Bulgars integrated (became absorbed) into Slavic society. They intermarried with Slavs and adopted the Slavic language and customs.

Asparukh, a Bulgar khan (prince), created the First Bulgarian Empire in 681. He set up his capital at the city of Pliska in northeastern Bulgaria. The new kingdom frequently warred with the Byzantine Empire. Under Khan Krum (called the Dreadful), the Bulgarians attacked Constantinople.

In 863 Khan Boris I converted to the Christian faith. He ordered his subjects to give up their ancient tribal religions and become Christians. After a disagreement with the pope, the leader of the Christian Church in Rome, Boris allied with the eastern Christian Church in Constantinople. This alliance reestablished Bulgaria's ties to the Byzantine Empire.

Bulgaria reached its peak under Czar (emperor) Simeon. During his reign (893–927), the kingdom grew to include modern-day Serbia, Albania, Macedonia, and parts of modern-day Romania. It was the most powerful nation in the Balkans. Trade, literature, and art flourished, and the kingdom grew rich. About this time, the nation adopted the Cyrillic alphabet, which was created by two Christian monks, brothers Cyril and Methodius.

Conquest and Rebellion

After Simeon's death in 927, Bulgaria began to weaken. Russians invaded from the north, and Byzantines invaded from the east. The Byzantine emperor Basil II, known as the Bulgar Slayer, defeated the

Bulgarian army in 1014. To prevent a counterattack, Basil ordered the blinding of fourteen thousand Bulgarian soldiers (by putting out their eyes). He then conquered the remaining Bulgarian lands and brought them into the Byzantine Empire.

The Byzantines ruled Bulgaria harshly and taxed the Bulgarians heavily. The nation's economy declined. The Bulgarians revolted several times without success. The region suffered further destruction in the twelfth century when Crusaders (Christian warriors) marched through Bulgaria on their way to the Middle East. The Crusaders demanded free food and shelter, stole crops and livestock, and ransacked farms and villages as they traveled.

Byzantine rule lasted until the 1180s, when two noblemen, brothers named Asen and Petâr, staged a successful rebellion. The brothers founded the Second Bulgarian Empire, with its capital at Veliko Turnovo in the Balkan Mountains. The empire expanded, first reclaiming Macedonia, then Albania and western modern-day Turkey. By the middle of the thirteenth century, Bulgaria again controlled much of the Balkan Peninsula. Its many seaports gave merchants easy access to foreign markets. Trade flourished, and the nation minted its first coins. Attracted by business opportunities, immigrants flocked to Bulgaria from other nations.

Bulgaria's nobles and merchants enjoyed rising prosperity. But while the wealthy prospered, Bulgaria's peasants suffered from poverty, hunger, and disease. They enjoyed few rights and paid high taxes to their landlords. In 1277 Bulgaria's peasants revolted, defeated the czar, and placed their own leader, Ivailo, on the throne. Then the empire declined again. Warriors from Serbia, the Middle East, and central Russia invaded the nation's borders.

In about 1300, the Ottoman Turks came to power in southwestern Asia. They set out to expand their territory, working east and west from their base in Anatolia (Turkey). In the 1360s, the Ottoman Turks invaded the Balkan Peninsula and attacked Bulgarian towns in the Maritsa River valley. In 1393 Veliko Turnovo, the Bulgarian capital, fell to the Turks. Three years later, the Ottoman Empire took over all of Bulgaria.

Ottoman Rule

After conquering the Balkan Peninsula, the Ottoman Turks controlled Bulgaria's economy and government. They seized Bulgarian farmland and turned it over to Turkish owners. Native Bulgarians had to work as serfs (laborers without land or freedom) for Turkish landlords. Many Bulgarian farmers fled into the surrounding mountains. Ottoman soldiers patrolled city streets and sometimes raped and robbed Bulgarian

The remains of the **Christ Pantocrator church,** built in the 1200s, is located in the medieval town of Nesebâr on the Black Sea. During their reign, the Ottomans punished Bulgaria's Christians. For links to more information on the history of religeon in Bulgaria, visit www.vgsbooks.com.

citizens. The Ottoman sultan levied heavy taxes on Bulgarians and stripped Bulgarian noblemen of their power.

The Ottomans, who followed the Islamic faith, also destroyed or looted many of Bulgaria's Christian churches. They tried to make Bulgarians convert to Islam. Those who agreed to convert (called Pomaks) did not have to pay taxes, and some of them gained important jobs in the Ottoman government. But those who refused to convert suffered harsh treatment. Many were killed. Hundreds of thousands fled the country during the Ottoman period, emigrating to neighboring Balkan nations.

Christian churches continued to operate in Bulgaria, but Bulgarian priests took their orders from church leaders in Constantinople (called Istanbul by the Ottomans, who conquered the city in 1453). Services were no longer conducted in Bulgarian but instead in Greek, the language used in Constantinople. Only in remote

SECOND-CLASS CITIZENS

During Ottoman rule, Christians faced intense discrimination. Among other restrictions, they were not allowed to ride horses, wear green (the color of Islam), or build their churches above a certain height.

mountain monasteries, far from Ottoman oversight, did Bulgarian priests continue to write and lead services in their own language.

The Bulgarian Revival

The Bulgarians staged several failed revolts against the Ottoman Turks. Gradually, however, the Ottoman Empire weakened. It could no longer tightly control Bulgarian society. In 1762 monk Paisii Hilendarski authored *The Slav-Bulgarian History*. This book, written in Bulgarian, celebrated Bulgarian culture and inspired Bulgarian people to oppose Ottoman rule. Teachers began to introduce students to Bulgarian art, folklore, and literature—much of it forgotten during the Ottoman era. New schools, libraries, and churches opened. Publishing houses printed new Bulgarian-language magazines and books. Influenced by trade with western Europe, Bulgarians opened new businesses. Some grew wealthy and built grand homes and buildings.

Meanwhile, the Russian Empire was expanding southward into the Balkan Peninsula. Russia, a Christian nation with a sizable Slavic population, felt strong cultural and religious ties to Bulgaria. In treaties signed in the late 1700s, the Russian czar pressed the Ottoman Turks to allow the Bulgarians greater religious and political freedom.

The expense of maintaining their huge realm further weakened the Ottoman Turks, who were facing revolts in Greece, Romania, and other occupied lands in the 1800s. In Bulgaria, revolutionary Georgi Rakovski led the movement for independence. Having already organized guerrilla bands (small groups of fighters) in Serbia and Romania, Rakovski trained a volunteer force to sweep across the Balkan Mountains and ignite a revolt in Bulgaria. Another guerrilla fighter, Vasil Levski, worked in Bulgarian villages to build an underground network of revolutionaries.

Vasil Levski helped fight for independence against the Ottoman Turks in the 1860s.

Russian soldiers cross the Balkan Mountains on their way to join forces with Bulgarian troops against the Ottomans.

At first, the Bulgarians failed. Rakovski died in 1867, and the Ottomans captured and executed Levski in 1873. Finally, other Bulgarians rose up against the Ottomans in April 1876. Ottoman troops suppressed the revolt with great cruelty—killing about thirty thousand Bulgarians and destroying nearly sixty villages. The Bulgarians then turned to Russia for help. Outraged by the killings, the Russian czar declared war in 1877 on the Ottoman Empire and ordered an invasion of the Balkans. Bulgarian and Russian soldiers defeated Ottoman forces in a series of fierce battles.

Dramatic Shipka Pass holds a special place in Bulgarian history. A strategic pathway between Kazanlâk and Gabrovo in the Sredna Gora, the pass was the site of an important victory for Macedonian conqueror Alexander the Great in 335 b.c. In August 1877, during a war between Russia and the Ottoman Empire, an army of only six thousand Russians and Bulgarians held off a force of twenty-seven thousand Ottomans at Shipka Pass.

In 1878 the Ottomans agreed to the Treaty of San Stefano. It stripped them of their European territories and gave most of the Balkan Peninsula back to Bulgaria. But many European nations feared that the fall of the Ottoman realm would lead to Russian domination of the Balkans. At the Congress of Berlin three months later, European nations changed the agreement, giving Macedonia and Thrace (part of southeastern Bulgaria) back to the Ottomans. They turned another portion of Bulgaria into a province called Eastern Rumelia, which remained under Ottoman control. The rest of Bulgaria became an independent principality (a region governed by a prince). It, too, remained under partial Ottoman control.

For links to more details about Ottoman rule and other historical imformation about Bulgaria, visit www.vgsbooks.com.

Independence

The Principality of Bulgaria adopted a constitution in 1879. The document established the Bulgarian National Assembly, or parliament, with members elected by a vote of adult male Bulgarian citizens. The parliament chose a prime minister to run the government, as well as a monarch (a prince or king) to serve as the nation's supreme leader. The National Assembly chose Alexander of Battenberg, a German prince and a nephew of the Russian czar, to become the Bulgarian monarch. Sofia, in western Bulgaria, became the new capital.

Hoping to increase his own power, Prince Alexander suspended (set aside) the new Bulgarian constitution. For several years, he ruled the country with the help of Russian military officers. Bulgaria suffered bitter disputes between liberals, who supported the constitution, and conservatives, who supported Alexander. Seeking to resolve the crisis, Alexander restored the constitution in 1883.

Two years later, the people of Eastern Rumelia revolted against the Ottoman Turks and joined their region to the Principality of Bulgaria. Alarmed at the growing power of Bulgaria, Russia backed a conspiracy to kidnap Alexander and to create a new Bulgarian government. Although the plot was discovered and never carried out, Alexander abdicated (gave up) the throne in 1886. Politician Stefan Stambolov stepped into the gap. Technically the prime minister but acting more like a dictator (a ruler with complete power), he was able to rid the government of Russian influence.

In 1894 the National Assembly elected another German, Prince Ferdinand, to rule as monarch. A capable and energetic leader, Ferdinand united the nation's political factions. Bulgaria modernized its industry and agriculture. The government built new schools, and literacy rates (numbers of people who could read and write) greatly increased. Factory workers organized the Social Democratic Party to fight for their interests. Peasants formed the Bulgarian Agrarian National Union. In 1908 Ferdinand (by then king) declared Bulgaria's complete independence from the Ottoman Empire.

King Ferdinand (second from right), his wife, and their two sons, Boris and Cyril, pose for a photograph.

War and Defeat

Despite their hard-won independence, Bulgarians were dissatisfied with the division of territory in the Balkan region. Still under Ottoman control, Thrace and Macedonia were home to large Bulgarian populations. Bulgaria's leaders wanted these territories in order to bring all Bulgarians into a single nation. The Bulgarians also wanted Thrace and Macedonia to improve trade and the economy, since these regions had ports on the Aegean Sea.

In 1912 Serbia, Bulgaria, and Greece formed an alliance and declared war on the Ottoman Turks. Bulgaria and its allies won the First Balkan War in 1913. But they could not agree on a division of territory. They all claimed Macedonia. This dispute led to the Second Balkan War. Bulgaria stood alone against its Balkan neighbors, this time joined by the Ottomans. Bulgaria quickly lost the second war. A treaty returned some Bulgarian land to the Ottoman Turks and awarded only a small portion of Macedonia to the Bulgarians.

By then rivalry over trade and territory had led Europe's nations to form two alliances. The Central powers consisted of Austria-Hungary, Germany, and the Ottoman Empire. The Allies contained Russia, Great Britain, Italy, and France. In the summer of 1914, a Serbian man assassinated a member of the Austrian royal family. Austria-Hungary then declared war on Serbia, an ally of Russia. The two alliances squared off against each other. The conflict, World War I (1914–1918), spread across Europe.

Bulgaria saw the war as an opportunity to reclaim its territory lost during the Second Balkan War. It sided with the Central powers, signing a treaty with Germany in 1915 that promised the return of Macedonia after the war. Bulgarian troops fought several battles that year against neighboring Serbia and Romania—both fighting with the Allies.

In the fall of 1918, the Central powers surrendered to the Allies. A treaty required Bulgaria to give up parts of Thrace and Macedonia to Greece. Bulgaria had to give up additional territory to the new Kingdom of the Serbs, Croats, and Slovenes (later called Yugoslavia). Angry at the defeat, the Bulgarian army threatened to revolt and seize power from King Ferdinand. To calm tensions, Ferdinand abdicated in favor of his son Boris III.

Postwar Turmoil

The end of the war brought chaos to Bulgaria. Unemployment grew, taxes were high, and inflation (rising prices) soared. Many rural families didn't have enough to eat. In the cities, poor and hungry factory workers went on strike to protest for government change.

In 1919 Alexandâr Stamboliiski, a leader of the Bulgarian Agrarian National Union, became prime minister. Stamboliiski's strongest support came from the country's peasants, who made up 80 percent of the population. His administration improved schools and changed Bulgaria's legal and tax systems to help the poor. The government also built new roads to improve trade and transportation and gave some land to peasants.

Divisions among the country's political groups continued, however. One prominent group was the Bulgarian Communist Party, an offshoot of the Social Democratic Party. The Communists favored state control of all business and the economy, with no private property. In Russia, Communists had overthrown their government during World War I, forming the Soviet Union in 1922. Fearing a similar overthrow in Bulgaria, many Bulgarian politicians and military officers opposed the Bulgarian Communists.

The Bulgarian economy continued to decline. Prices rose and workers continued to strike. Militants seeking self-rule for Macedonia struck out against the Bulgarian government with killings and other violence. Communists and conservatives battled in the streets of Sofia. Though popular with peasants, Stamboliiski was unpopular with city dwellers and the armed forces. In 1923 a group of conservative politicians and army officers formed the Military League, a secret organization that assassinated him.

After Stamboliiski's death, a civil war broke out between Bulgaria's political factions. The conservatives, allied with the military, eventually prevailed. The new government arrested and imprisoned many of its opponents and outlawed the Communist Party. Alarmed by the growing power of the military, King Boris III took control of the government in

Boris III (*left*) ruled Bulgaria during much of World War II. Boris died in August 1943. His six-year-old son, Simeon II, replaced him on the throne.

1935. He forced the prime minister out of office and declared a royal dictatorship, giving himself absolute power. He tried to weaken the conservatives and the military and restore balance to government.

World War II

During the 1930s, new regimes took power in Italy and Germany. In 1936 the two nations formed a military alliance called the Axis. Under Adolf Hitler, the leader of the Nazi Party, Germany denounced the treaties that had ended World War I and rearmed. Trade between Bulgaria and Germany brought the two countries closer together. King Boris also formed ties with Italy by marrying Princess Giovanna, the daughter of the Italian king.

Adolf Hitler

When Germany invaded Poland in the summer of 1939, Britain and France immediately declared war on Germany. World War II soon spread throughout Europe, including the Balkan nations. At first, Bulgaria declared itself neutral (not taking sides) in the war, but under increasing pressure from Germany, it joined the Axis in 1941. The nations fighting the Axis—France, Great Britain, the Soviet Union, the United States, and others—were called the Allies.

Despite their ties to Germany, the Bulgarians—who remembered Russia's help in the fight for Bulgarian independence—refused to join a German attack on the Soviet Union in the summer of 1942. Bulgaria escaped much of the war's destruction until 1943, when Allied air forces bombed Sofia and other cities. As weakening German forces retreated in September 1944, Bulgaria sought peace with the Allies, but before a deal was struck, Soviet forces driving into the Balkan Peninsula occupied Bulgaria.

In addition to defeating the Axis, the Soviets wanted to spread their Communist form of government throughout Eastern Europe. In Bulgaria, Soviet forces arrested existing government officials and allowed the Fatherland Front, a coalition of Bulgarian Communists and other parties, to seize power.

Although called an independent nation, Bulgaria quickly became a satellite of the Soviet Union. The Soviet Union set all foreign and economic policy for Bulgaria and insisted that the nation follow Communist principles and practices. (The Soviets also set up Communist governments in East Germany, Hungary, Poland, and Romania after the war.)

◉ Communist Rule

The Communists quickly took control of the Fatherland Front and killed or imprisoned many of their political opponents. In 1946 the new Communist-led government held a vote that abolished the monarchy and established the People's Republic of Bulgaria. The royal family, including the new king, Simeon II (then only nine years old), fled the country. Georgi Dimitrov, a leader of the Bulgarian Communists, became the country's new prime minister.

Under Dimitrov's direction, the government wrote a new constitution modeled on that of the Soviet Union.

THE SOVIET BLOC

In the wake of World War II, the Soviet Union set up Communist governments in Bulgaria, East Germany, Hungary, Poland, and Romania. Communist governments developed without Soviet involvement in Albania, Yugoslavia, and Czechoslovakia.

The Communist nations of Eastern Europe were called the Soviet bloc or Soviet satellites. Although the nations claimed to be independent, they were really controlled by the Soviet Union. The Soviets dictated their foreign and economic policies. Their educational, employment, and other social systems were all based on the Soviet model. The nations of the Soviet bloc broke off trade with the West and primarily did business with one another.

In the late 1980s, the nations of Eastern Europe, as well as the Soviet Union, began to cast off Communism and establish free, democratic governments. In 1991 the Soviet Union broke apart into fifteen independent states. The fall of the Soviet Union and other Communist governments put an end to the Soviet bloc.

Under the new system, a small group of Communist Party leaders controlled the entire government. Other political parties were banned. The government took over businesses, churches, and the media. It greatly restricted people's rights, such as free speech and freedom of assembly. It seized private property, such as factories, and put businesses under state control. Factory workers became government employees. The government also took over small farms and grouped them into larger, state-run collective farms.

In 1950 Vulko Chervenkov became the head of the Bulgarian Communist Party. Chervenkov strengthened ties with the Soviet Union and cut off Bulgaria's trade with the nations of Western Europe. The government assumed even greater control over people's lives—even dictating what sort of art could be created. People who spoke out against the government were sent to labor camps to be punished, starved, and sometimes worked to death.

Todor Zhivkov became head of state in 1962 and ruled for the next three decades. During the early years of Zhivkov's rule, Bulgaria's economy stagnated (stood still). State-controlled factories and farms did not run efficiently. Food, consumer goods, and housing became increasingly scarce, and people grew poor. But Zhivkov later made reforms that improved the Bulgarian economy. In the 1970s, he reestablished ties to the nations of Western Europe. He allowed some

Bulgaria's Communist government built **high-rise concrete apartment buildings** in Sofia throughout the mid-1900s to house an influx of workers and their families from rural areas. The government gave these buildings names such as Youth, Friendship, and Hope. But the buildings were drab and dreary. In modern times, many of these Communist-era high-rises remain in use.

foreign businesses to invest in Bulgaria, improved industrial technology, and loosened government control over business. The nation's economy improved somewhat.

Visit www.lernerbooks.com for details about Communist rule in Bulgaria.

Communism Falls

In Communist nations such as Bulgaria, the government guaranteed people jobs, schooling, and health care—but very little freedom. Many people in Bulgaria, the Soviet Union, and other Communist nations were unhappy with this form of government. They wanted the kinds of rights and freedoms that people enjoyed in Western Europe and the United States.

In 1989, in Bulgaria and other Communist countries, discontented citizens demonstrated in the streets and formed underground political

A demonstrator takes a stand in 1989 in front of the Aleksandâr Nevski Church, a Sofia landmark. He holds a sign demanding an end to King Simeon II's exile from Bulgaria. Bulgaria's royal family had fled the country in 1946.

A demonstrator holds a leaflet featuring Petâr Mladenov at this 1989 prodemocracy rally in Sofia.

parties. Weakened by its own internal problems, the Soviet Union could not prevent the downfall of Communist governments in several Eastern European nations. In Bulgaria the Communists fought among themselves. Foreign minister Petâr Mladenov led a group of fellow Communists in a coup (takeover) that forced Zhivkov from office in November 1989.

Responding to popular pressure, Mladenov's Communist government then agreed to give up absolute power in favor of multiparty elections. The first election, in June 1990, pitted the Communists, renamed the Bulgarian Socialist Party (BSP), against the newly formed Union of Democratic Forces (UDF). The BSP prevailed and retained power, but the UDF made a strong showing in the election and won the following year.

Throughout the early 1990s, government control seesawed back and forth between the BSP and the UDF. Meanwhile, the government began to dismantle the state-controlled economy and to establish a free-market economic system like that used in the United States. Bulgaria sold state industries to private business and turned over farmland to individual farmers—sometimes to people who had owned the land before the Communist era.

Simeon II, the former king of Bulgaria, casts his ballot in the 2001 national election. As the successful candidate for prime minister that year, he became the first former monarch in Eastern Europe to come to power in a democracy.

The transition proved to be tough. In 1996, with the BSP in power, the economy plummeted. Inflation and unemployment soared. Fuel and food were scarce. Some businesspeople ignored laws and regulations, cheating customers for their own gain. Other businesses traded in weapons and illegal drugs. Some government officials accepted bribes and favors from dishonest businessowners. To make matters worse, nearby Yugoslavia became engulfed in a bloody civil war in the 1990s. The conflict hurt trade throughout the Balkans. Bulgaria's economy slumped even further.

The UDF took power again in 1997 and made changes. New leaders cracked down on crooked businesses and corrupt government officials. They passed new tax and banking laws and halted runaway inflation. In 2001 Simeon II, Bulgaria's former king who had left Bulgaria as a boy, returned from exile to become prime minister. With his National Movement Simeon II Party, he enacted more economic reforms, such as raising the minimum wage for workers.

◉ Joining the West

In the early 2000s, Bulgaria also became involved in major international events. In 2003, as part of its "war on terrorism," the United States invaded the Middle Eastern nation of Iraq. U.S. president

George W. Bush said the invasion was necessary because the United States suspected that Iraq had "weapons of mass destruction" (nuclear, chemical, and biological weapons) and was planning to use them against other nations. The president also wanted to topple Iraq's cruel dictator, Saddam Hussein, and to set up a new, democratic government in Iraq.

The United States asked for nations around the world to join in a coalition (alliance) to fight in Iraq. Bulgarian leaders wanted to help fight against terrorism. They also saw the benefits of aligning themselves with the powerful United States. So in spring 2003, along with about fifty other countries, Bulgaria joined the war in Iraq. Bulgarian leaders also offered to allow the United States to build military bases in Bulgaria in the future.

Bulgaria sent a force of about five hundred infantrymen (foot soldiers) to Iraq. The

In 2004 Iraqi insurgents captured two Bulgarian civilian truck drivers working in Iraq. The insurgents threatened to kill the men if the U.S. military did not release Iraqi prisoners. Both the Bulgarian and U.S. governments refused to give in to the insurgents' demands, and both Bulgarians were soon killed. The killings shocked and saddened Bulgarians, but it did not weaken their resolve to assist the United States in its fight in Iraq.

The mother of one of the Bulgarian truck drivers killed by Iraqi insurgents cries over his coffin as she holds his picture.

The flag-draped coffin of a Bulgarian soldier killed in Karbala, Iraq, hoisted by a Bulgarian army color guard, arrives at the Sofia airport in December 2003.

soldiers guarded Iraqi cities from insurgents, or fighters who were resisting coalition forces. The Bulgarian troops also patrolled cities and buildings to make the streets safe for the Iraqi people. Some Bulgarian civilians (nonmilitary citizens) also went to Iraq. They took jobs rebuilding war-damaged schools, streets, and buildings and helping Iraqis create a new democratic society. At least six Bulgarian soldiers and two Bulgarian civilians were killed during the war.

Bulgaria made another military alliance on March 29, 2004, when it joined the North Atlantic Treaty Organization (NATO). NATO, a coalition of twenty-six nations, includes the United States and the nations of Western Europe. As part of NATO, Bulgaria will continue its involvement in the war on terrorism and other international military efforts.

Government

The fall of Bulgaria's Communist regime transformed the nation's government. In 1990 Bulgaria held its first multiparty elections since the end of World War II. The following year, it created a new constitution.

All Bulgarian citizens older than eighteen are eligible to vote. They elect a president for a five-year term. The president com-

Bulgaria's National Assembly meets in this building.

mands the nation's armed forces and has many formal duties, such as representing the nation to foreign leaders. Voters also elect members of parliament, called the National Assembly. The assembly has 240 members with four-year terms. The majority party (party with the most seats) in the National Assembly chooses a prime minister, who appoints a cabinet, or group of advisers. The prime minister and cabinet are responsible for overall government operations.

Bulgaria is divided into twenty-eight provinces, which handle matters of local government. These provinces are further divided into smaller districts. Within provinces and districts, people elect government officials.

Courts operate at each level of government—from the district to the national level. The highest court in the nation is the Supreme Judicial Council. The council hears appeals from lower courts and rules on constitutional questions.

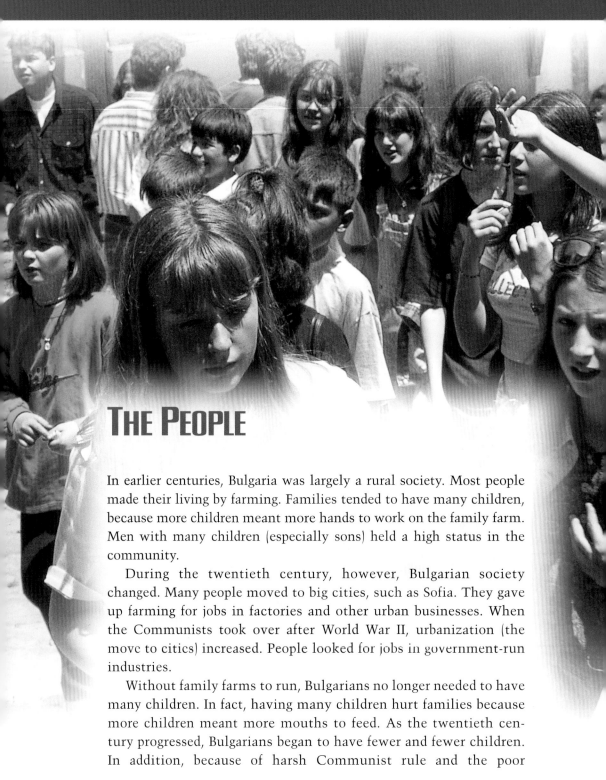

THE PEOPLE

In earlier centuries, Bulgaria was largely a rural society. Most people made their living by farming. Families tended to have many children, because more children meant more hands to work on the family farm. Men with many children (especially sons) held a high status in the community.

During the twentieth century, however, Bulgarian society changed. Many people moved to big cities, such as Sofia. They gave up farming for jobs in factories and other urban businesses. When the Communists took over after World War II, urbanization (the move to cities) increased. People looked for jobs in government-run industries.

Without family farms to run, Bulgarians no longer needed to have many children. In fact, having many children hurt families because more children meant more mouths to feed. As the twentieth century progressed, Bulgarians began to have fewer and fewer children. In addition, because of harsh Communist rule and the poor

economy, many people left Bulgaria for other nations during the Communist era. Population growth slowed. Then overall population figures declined.

The trends continued even after the Communists left office in 1989. Many couples had only one child. Bulgarians, especially young people, left the nation to look for a better life. In 1990 the Bulgarian population stood at nearly 9 million. By 2000 the population had fallen to under 8 million, and by 2003 it was estimated at 7.5 million.

Bulgaria's population does not show signs of increasing. Many Bulgarian couples would like to have two or more children, but they can't afford to raise them. Statistically, the typical Bulgarian woman will have only 1 child in her lifetime. Bulgarians use birth control and abortion (legal in early pregnancy and to save the life of the mother) to limit the size of their families. The country's population density—187 people per square mile (72 people per sq. km)—is one of the lowest in Europe.

RURAL AND URBAN LIFE

Most of Bulgaria's 7.5 million people live in urban areas. Life in urban Bulgaria is much like life in American and Western European cities. Cars, buses, and people on foot crowd city streets. People work in factories, shops, and office buildings. They enjoy nightclubs, cafés, and restaurants. They generally wear Western-style clothing.

Rural Bulgaria tends to have a slower pace than urban Bulgaria. Many people in the countryside still make a living by farming. Many farmers transport goods by horse-drawn carts. Bulgaria's small towns are quiet and sparsely populated. Many rural people live in centuries-old stone and timber farmhouses. Some churches, monasteries, and other rural buildings are more than 1,500 years old.

◎ Health Care

During the Communist era, Bulgarians benefited from extensive social services. The government ran hospitals and health clinics, paid for citizens' health care, and gave workers sick leave and disability pay. Elderly people got pensions (pay and health care benefits) when they retired. Bulgaria's health system suffered from inefficiency, however. Many doctors (who were government employees) were underpaid and poorly trained. Patients had to wait a long time for care.

With the fall of Communism, Bulgaria's social service system underwent big changes. To save money, the government cut back or eliminated some health programs. Doctors became free to open private medical practices. When the economy suffered in the early 1990s, health care suffered as well. Prices for medicines and health care soared. Some common medicines, including aspirin, were scarce. Compounding the problem, many Bulgarians smoked, drank alcohol heavily, and ate sugary and fatty foods—eating habits that contribute to illnesses such as heart disease and cancer. In some industrial areas, people suffered from respiratory (breathing) problems, caused by air pollution. Many people died in middle age.

To improve health care for its people, the Bulgarian government made reforms in the 1990s. It borrowed money from international agencies such as the World Bank, then used the money to strengthen hospitals and health services. Some doctors studied abroad, learning up-to-date techniques at foreign medical schools.

In the twenty-first century, the Bulgarian government provides some free health care to citizens, while doctors also run private medical offices. The nation has about 350 doctors and 700 nurses for every 100,000 people, numbers roughly equal to those found in the United

A Bulgarian Red Cross worker holds a candle at a **candlelight vigil** in honor of World AIDS Day on December 1, 2004. For links to websites with health and population statistics for Bulgaria, visit www.vgsbooks.com.

States and Western European nations. The infant mortality rate (numbers of infants who die at or near birth) is fairly low, at 14 deaths per 1,000 births. Life expectancy is 68 years for men and 75 years for women. Bulgaria also has a low HIV infection rate. (HIV, or human immunodeficiency virus, is the virus that causes AIDS, or acquired immunodeficiency syndrome.) Infection rates are reported at less than 0.1 percent of the adult population.

While the Bulgarian health care system is fairly good and improving, it is not equal in quality to the care in the United States or Western European nations. Bulgarian doctors don't always have up-to-date equipment or a wide range of medicines to treat patients. The best care is found in Sofia and other big cities.

Well into the twentieth century, most people in Bulgaria relied on traditional healers for health care. Healers used natural treatments, such as herbs and other plants, to treat illness. Some people thought that evil spirits could cause sickness, so healers also treated illnesses using magic and chants. The tradition of herbal healing continues. In fact, most Bulgarian towns have a *bilkova apteka*, or herbal pharmacy, selling natural remedies.

Education

Education has long played an important role in Bulgarian life. In earlier centuries, most education took place in churches and monasteries, where students (only men) learned to read and write religious texts. During the National Revival of the 1800s, schooling became more widespread. The curriculum expanded beyond religious studies to include literature, arithmetic, and other subjects. In 1878 the Bulgarian government established free elementary schools for both boys and girls. Many children did not attend school, however, especially in rural areas, because their parents needed them to work on the family farm.

Education expanded even more during the Communist era. The government opened new schools and universities. It wanted as many citizens as possible to learn to read and write and to complete high school. The government used the school system to teach citizens about Communism and to inspire loyalty to the Communist Party. Teachers had to be Communist Party members. As part of their education, students learned Russian, the language of the Soviet Union. They also learned skills in preparation for jobs in state-owned factories and other businesses.

Bulgarian schools changed again after Communism fell. Modern-day students no longer study Russian or learn about Communism in school. The modern curriculum includes history, science, mathematics, grammar, and languages. Many students learn English in school. Some students attend high schools that emphasize job training, while others attend special schools for language, music, or religion. School is mandatory (required) for children ages seven to sixteen.

Bulgaria has more than twenty universities and colleges, including the well-respected University of Sofia. The American University of Bulgaria, opened in the early 1990s in Blagoevgrad, offers students an American-style, English-language education. Some young Bulgarians attend college in foreign countries.

The emphasis on education has paid off for Bulgaria. Its literacy rate (percentage of people who can read and write) is extremely high. According to government figures, 99 percent of men and 98 percent of women are literate.

Ethnic Groups

Bulgaria is home to several ethnic groups. The largest group is the ethnic Bulgarians, descendants of the early Slavs and Bulgars. Ethnic Bulgarians make up 84 percent of the population. They live scattered throughout the nation—in both small towns and big cities. Most ethnic Bulgarians are Christians.

Turkish Bulgarian youths swim in the Danube River at Nikopol, Bulgaria. The Turnu Magurele Chemical Plant in Romania can be seen across the river.

Turks—descendants of Turkish immigrants who arrived during the Ottoman era—make up almost 10 percent of the Bulgarian population. Most Bulgarian Turks live in northeastern Bulgaria and in the eastern Rhodope Mountains. Turkish Bulgarians generally practice the Islamic faith. As recently as the late 1980s, the Bulgarian government discriminated against the Turks. But in modern Bulgaria, Turks enjoy the same rights and freedoms as other ethnic groups. A Turkish political party, the Movement for Rights and Freedoms, was formed in 1990.

Roma people, or Rom, account for about 5 percent of Bulgaria's population. Also called gypsies, the Rom originated in northern India. About A.D. 1000, they began leaving India, traveling through various foreign

TROUBLE FOR TURKS

In the early 1980s, when the Communists were still in power, the Bulgarian government discriminated against Turks. The government forced them to take Bulgarian names, shut down mosques, and banned the Turkish language and Turkish clothing styles. Bulgarian Turks who refused to cooperate lost their jobs or houses or were sent to labor camps. Many Turks protested, and several hundred thousand left Bulgaria for Turkey. The oppressive laws were lifted in 1989, and many Turks returned.

A Roma mother and daughter stand in a field of flowers.

lands. Many Rom settled in the Balkans. In Bulgaria, Roma communities are found in the Valley of the Roses, the city of Sliven, and other major cities. Most Rom practice the Islamic faith and speak the Romany language. Like the Turks, Bulgaria's Roma people have been victims of discrimination. They tend to be among the poorest people in Bulgaria, with high rates of unemployment. Many live in all-Rom ghettos in big cities. The rest of Bulgaria's population— approximately 2 percent—is made up of other ethnic groups, including Armenians and Macedonians.

Changing Roles for Women

Bulgarian society changed dramatically in the twentieth century, and the status of Bulgarian women changed as well. In traditional, rural Bulgarian society, women held second-class status. They were expected to obey their husbands and have many children. They did housework and farmwork but did not hold jobs outside the home.

With Communism, women's roles changed greatly. Under Communism, the state guaranteed a job for everyone—male and female. Women were generally given low-level cleaning, secretarial, and sales jobs. Men held positions of authority. But there were some positives to the system. For instance, the government paid men and women equally for the same jobs and provided child care to working mothers.

When Communism ended, Bulgaria entered a free-market economy. Citizens were no longer guaranteed jobs. As the economy struggled in the 1990s, many Bulgarians couldn't find work and still cannot. Unemployment among women is three times higher than among men. Men are usually paid more than women for the same jobs. With few employment options, some Bulgarian women are forced into prostitution to earn a living. Other issues facing modern Bulgarian women are sexual abuse and domestic violence.

 Visit www. vgsbooks.com for links to websites about the diverse peoples of Bulgaria.

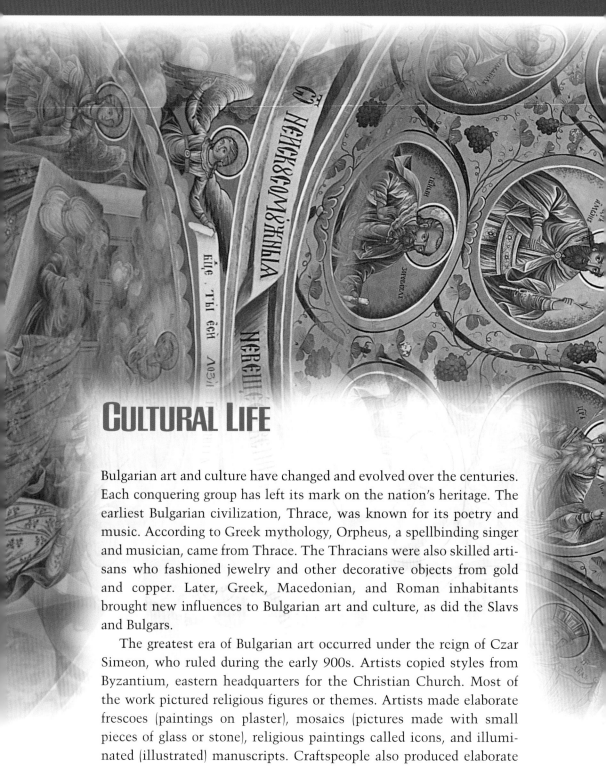

CULTURAL LIFE

Bulgarian art and culture have changed and evolved over the centuries. Each conquering group has left its mark on the nation's heritage. The earliest Bulgarian civilization, Thrace, was known for its poetry and music. According to Greek mythology, Orpheus, a spellbinding singer and musician, came from Thrace. The Thracians were also skilled artisans who fashioned jewelry and other decorative objects from gold and copper. Later, Greek, Macedonian, and Roman inhabitants brought new influences to Bulgarian art and culture, as did the Slavs and Bulgars.

The greatest era of Bulgarian art occurred under the reign of Czar Simeon, who ruled during the early 900s. Artists copied styles from Byzantium, eastern headquarters for the Christian Church. Most of the work pictured religious figures or themes. Artists made elaborate frescoes (paintings on plaster), mosaics (pictures made with small pieces of glass or stone), religious paintings called icons, and illuminated (illustrated) manuscripts. Craftspeople also produced elaborate

woodcarvings, jewelry, carpets, and embroidered clothing, while architects created grand domed churches.

When the Ottomans conquered Bulgaria in the 1300s, Bulgarian artistry faded away. The Ottomans imposed the Islamic religion and culture on Bulgaria. Bulgarians were not allowed to produce religious-themed paintings and other artwork. The Ottomans destroyed many splendid Bulgarian churches, monasteries, and works of art. They replaced them with their own mosques and religious symbols.

In the 1800s, Bulgaria entered its National Revival period. Then Ottoman influence weakened, and the Bulgarians revived long-dormant arts. Zahari Zograf, a leading National Revival painter, created striking frescoes in churches and monasteries. Other painters depicted scenes of rural Bulgarian life. In the cities, Bulgarians began to build ornate homes, with tiled roofs, elaborate woodwork, and bright interior murals. Textile arts from the Byzantine era, such as embroidery, weaving, and carpet making, flourished again.

Artistic freedom continued into the twentieth century. But after World War II, Bulgaria became a Communist nation. The Communist Party drew up strict guidelines for artists, writers, filmmakers, and composers. Visual artists had to work in the Socialist Realism style, designed to glorify Communism. Socialist Realist works often featured images of noble farmers and factory workers, laboring to build a strong Communist society. Sculptors erected Socialist Realist works in public squares and buildings throughout Bulgaria. Many Bulgarian artists trained in the Soviet Union.

With the fall of the Communist Party in Bulgaria, artists again became free to create any kind of artwork. In the twenty-first century, Bulgarian artists exhibit their works in Bulgaria and around the world. Artists include Rumen Rachev, with his boldly colorful paintings, and Bora Nikolaeva Petkova, who makes eerie human sculptures. Perhaps the best-known Bulgarian artist is Christo Javacheff, internationally famous for his vast outdoor sculptures. Known by the name Christo, this artist was born in Bulgaria in 1935. He moved to Paris and then New York as a young man.

The seventeenth-century Pont Neuf, a bridge in Paris, France, was the object of one of Bulgarian-born Christo's outdoor sculpture projects. He wrapped the bridge in nylon fabric in September 1985. The project used 439,985 square feet (40,876 sq. m) of fabric and 42,900 feet (13,075 m) of rope.

The **Bulgarian State Female Vocal Choir** delights audiences with its astounding harmonies.

Music and Dance

The ancient Thracians, particularly the mythical Orpheus, were skillful musicians. Over the centuries, Bulgarians created folk songs and dances. They made instruments, such as the *gayda,* a goatskin bagpipe; the tamboura, a four-stringed instrument similar to a lute; and the *kaval,* a type of wooden flute. Many modern musicians play old Bulgarian folk tunes on these and other traditional instruments.

Dancers stand either in a circle or a straight line to perform a popular Bulgarian folk dance, the *horo.* This quick-tempo dance has many variations. Dancers usually hold onto one another's belts as they dance. Some dancers wave handkerchiefs.

Bulgarian women have a unique singing style, passed down from mothers to daughters. The style features a chorus of singers whose voices rise and fall in astounding harmonies. In the 1980s, the sound attracted international audiences. Bulgarian women's choirs performed to sold-out crowds in the United States and elsewhere. The Bulgarian State Female Vocal Choir even won Grammy awards in 1988 and 1990. The group's *The Mystery of Bulgarian Voices* (volumes 1 and 2) was named the best traditional folk recording.

Opera is popular in Bulgaria. The country has several opera theaters. The best and most famous is the National Opera House in Sofia. Boris Christoff, Gena Dimitrova, Anna Tomova-Sintova, and others are world-famous Bulgarian opera singers. Bulgarians also enjoy pop, jazz, rock, and other modern music. Kaval player Teodossi Spassov performs a fusion of traditional Bulgarian folk music and jazz.

Language and Literature

Bulgaria's official language is Bulgarian, although people speak other languages, including Turkish, Armenian, and Greek. Some people also speak English.

Bulgarian, an ancient Slavic tongue, is related to Russian. The language came to Bulgaria with the Slavs in the fifth century. The Bulgars, who arrived a century or so later, adopted this language. People in early Bulgaria spoke other languages, including Greek and Turkish, but the Bulgars came to dominate the country and the language.

Bulgarian uses the Cyrillic alphabet, a writing system created in the ninth century A.D. by the brothers Cyril and Methodius. These Christian missionaries (religious teachers) were born in Macedonia. They devised Cyrillic to write the Bible and other religious works in the language of the common people. Bulgarian Cyrillic has twenty-nine letters. Some of them look nothing like the letters used to write English.

An icon in the sixteenth-century Trojan Monastery near Trojan, Bulgaria, depicts the likenesses of **Cyril and Methodius.** The saints invented the Cyrillic alphabet in the ninth century A.D.

Most early Bulgarian writing was religious. During the Ottoman era, the Bulgarian church took orders from church leaders in Constantinople (renamed Istanbul in 1453). These leaders didn't allow Bulgarian-language schools, writings, or church services. Only Greek, the official language of the church, could be used. That changed in the late 1700s with the dawning of the Bulgarian National Revival. Father Paisii Hilendarski, a monk, wrote *The Slav-Bulgarian History* (1762), inspiring Bulgarians to reclaim their national heritage. Soon after, Bulgarians began opening Bulgarian-language schools, libraries, and publishing companies. People began to enjoy old and new Bulgarian songs, folktales, and literature.

A FEW BULGARIAN WORDS AND THEIR MEANINGS

banya: a public sauna or spa
gora: forest
grad: a city or town
khan: a title used by early Bulgarian rulers
kilim: a woolen carpet with an intricate design inside a border
planina: mountain
ploshtad: a town square
stara: old
tsârkva: church
veliko: great

The writers Hristo Botev and Ivan Vazov fanned the flames of revolution against Turkey in the late 1800s. Botev spoke out against the Ottomans, using impassioned poems and newspaper articles. Vazov was a novelist. His *Under the Yoke*, which gained an international audience, described the harsh conditions endured by Bulgarians during Ottoman rule. After independence, Yordan Yovkov, Dimiter Dimov, and others wrote about the lives of ordinary people in rural Bulgaria.

Under Communist rule, the government tightly restricted the style and subjects of published works. The Communist Party closely supervised writers' unions and the publication of books, newspapers, and magazines. Writings that criticized Communism or the government were not allowed. The government sometimes jailed writers who broke the rules. Some writers left Bulgaria for nations that allowed artistic freedom.

After Communism fell in Bulgaria, writers were again able to express themselves freely. They founded new publishing houses, journals, and newspapers. Modern Bulgaria has a thriving literary scene. Companies such as Balkani Publishing and Edelweiss Books and Periodicals distribute the best in Bulgarian literature to readers around the world. One of Bulgaria's most acclaimed contemporary writers, Blaga Dimitrova, a poet, playwright, essayist, and novelist, died in 2003.

An outdoor sign in Sofia advertises cell phone service.

Modern Media

Bulgaria is "wired" with the usual modern communications—faxes, cell phones, e-mail, cable TV, and the Internet. About 150 Internet service providers operate in Bulgaria. Almost every town has at least one Internet café. In 2001 about 500,000 Bulgarians had Internet service, and more than 1 million had cell phones—numbers that are growing quickly. Landline telephone service is not available everywhere in Bulgaria, however. Especially in rural areas, service can be limited.

Since the fall of Communism, Bulgaria has enjoyed freedom of the press, and Bulgarians are eager to express their opinions through the media. The nation has about one hundred radio stations and nearly forty television stations that broadcast both Bulgarian- and foreign-produced programs. Daily newspapers in Bulgaria include *Trud* (Work), *24 Chasa* (24 Hours), *Demokratsiya* (Democracy), *Dnevnik* (Journal), and *Kapital* (Capital). Hundreds of other newspapers come out less frequently. The nation also has a small film industry producing fictional and documentary works. Occasionally, foreign film companies shoot movies in Bulgaria, particularly in the picturesque Rhodope Mountains.

Religion

The Thracians, Romans, Slavs, and other early inhabitants of Bulgaria worshiped a variety of deities (gods and goddesses). Often their religious ceremonies centered on basic needs for survival, such as asking the gods for a good harvest or a successful hunt. In 865 Czar Boris converted his empire to Christianity. He built churches and monasteries and required people to give up pagan (non-Christian) religious practices. The Christian church flourished in Bulgaria for several hundred years afterward.

Bulgaria has 160 monasteries. Monasteries are religious communities whose members, called monks (men) and nuns (women), have devoted their lives to God. Some of the monasteries are open to visitors.

The Ottoman Turks took over Bulgaria in the late 1300s. The conquering Turks practiced the Islamic religion and forced many Bulgarians to convert to Islam. After the Ottomans lost control of Bulgaria, Christianity grew strong once again. After the Ottomans left, some followers of Islam (some Turkish, some converted Bulgarians) remained in Bulgaria. The nation was also home to small communities of Roman Catholics, Jews, and Protestants.

By World War II, about fifty thousand Jews were living in Bulgaria. The Germans had passed anti-Jewish laws in their own nation. They then deported millions of European Jews to concentration camps, where most of them were killed. Germany demanded that its ally, Bulgaria, take similar actions against Bulgarian Jews. At first, the Bulgarian government complied. It sent the Jews of Bulgarian-controlled Macedonia and Thrace to German-run concentration camps. But bolstered by widespread support for the Jews at home, the government refused to hand over the Jews of Bulgaria. Instead, it sent Jews to labor camps inside Bulgaria, where they were imprisoned but not killed. After the war, nearly 90 percent of Bulgaria's Jews immigrated to Israel, the Jewish homeland in the Middle East.

During the Communist era, the Bulgarian government strictly controlled religious organizations, primarily the Bulgarian Orthodox Church, the nation's dominant church. The government shut down some churches. It kept priests under close surveillance (watch). It jailed priests who spoke out against government policies. The government frowned upon religious schools, writings, rituals, and holidays such as Christmas. However, most Bulgarians practiced their religion quietly, and the Christian church remained important in everyday life.

With the fall of Communism in 1990, Bulgaria's government lifted all restrictions on religious practice. New churches and religious schools were opened. Church rituals and holidays again took a prominent role in Bulgaria. Bulgaria's 1991 constitution guarantees freedom of religion for all citizens.

The Orthodox **Aleksander Nevsky Church** in Sofia was completed in 1912. It was built to honor the Russian czar who helped liberate Bulgaria from Turkish rule in the late 1700s.

Most Bulgarians belong to the Bulgarian Orthodox Church, an independent branch of the Eastern Orthodox Church. Armenian, Russian, and Greek Orthodox churches also operate in Bulgaria. In all, about 84 percent of Bulgarians are Orthodox Christians, although only some regularly attend church.

About 12 percent of Bulgaria's people are Muslims—people who practice Islam, a religion founded on the Arabian Peninsula in the seventh century A.D. Most Bulgarian Muslims are ethnic Turks (descendants of the Ottoman conquerors). Others, called Pomaks, are descendants of Bulgarians who converted to Islam during the Ottoman era.

About 2 percent of Bulgarians are Roman Catholic. Less than 1 percent of Bulgarians is Jewish. The remaining 1 percent is Protestant (non-Catholic Christians), belong to another religious group, or do not practice any religion.

 For links to websites with more information on religious practices in Bulgaria, visit www.vgsbooks.com.

Holidays and Festivals

Like people in all nations, Bulgarians observe many holidays. Christians honor Christian holidays, while Muslims mark their own holidays, including the holy month of Ramadan.

Bulgarians also hold festivals and other celebrations throughout the year. Many are folk festivals, featuring traditional songs, dances, and costumes. The Koprivshtitsa Folklore Festival, held every five years, is the largest and most famous. The Festival of the Roses, held in Kazanlâk and Karlovo in June, celebrates the roses grown in the region. Festivalgoers can enjoy rose jam, rose brandy, and other rose products, including magical-smelling rose oil. Weddings, christenings (baby namings), and birthdays are all causes for celebration in Bulgaria. Saint days (to honor Orthodox Christian saints) are also times for a party, especially for people named after the saint being honored. Bulgarian celebrations usually include plenty of dancing and good food, especially bread.

On official Bulgarian holidays, government offices and many businesses shut down. There are ten official holidays. New Year's Day is January 1. Liberation Day, commemorating Bulgaria's initial break from the Turks in 1878, is March 3. Easter, the holiest day for Christians, falls in March or April. Labor Day, honoring workers, is May 1. Saint George's Day, celebrating the spring farming season, is May 6. May 24 is Bulgarian Education and Culture and Slavonic Literature Day, celebrating Bulgarian culture. September 6 is Unification Day, honoring the reunification of Bulgaria and Eastern Rumelia in 1885. Bulgarian Independence Day, September 22,

IN SHEEP'S CLOTHING

Kukeri celebrations, a tradition dating to pre-Christian times in Bulgaria, are held early in the year. Bulgarian men transform themselves into fantastic-looking creatures. They dress from head to toe in sheepskins, scary masks, and towering headdresses. Accompanied by drummers, they perform frenzied dances meant to drive away evil spirits.

A tough-looking bunch of Bulgarian kukeri dancers performs at a celebration that originated in pre-Christian times. Visit www.vgsbooks.com for more information on Bulgaria's holiday practices.

marks Bulgaria's 1908 independence from Turkey. National Revival Day, commemorating the resurgence of Bulgarian pride and identity, is November 1. December 24, 25, and 26 are days to celebrate Christmas.

FETA CHEESE AND POTATO PATTIES

1 pound Yukon gold potatoes

4 ounces feta cheese

4 scallions, chopped

1 tablespoon dried dill

1 tablespoon lemon juice

1 egg, beaten slightly

½ teaspoon salt

1 pinch pepper

1 cup flour for dredging (more if desired)

4 tablespoons canola oil

1. Boil the potatoes in their skins in salted water until easily pierced with a fork or the tip of a knife, approximately 15 to 30 minutes.
2. Peel potatoes while still warm and mash them in a bowl.
3. Crumble the feta cheese into the bowl.
4. Add scallions, dill, lemon juice, and egg.
5. Add salt and pepper and stir well.
6. Cover mixture with plastic wrap and refrigerate until firm.
7. Mold the mixture into walnut-sized balls, flatten them slightly, and dredge in flour.
8. Heat oil on medium heat in a large skillet.
9. Fry a batch of patties (as many as will fit in the skillet) in oil until golden brown on one side, approximately 3 to 5 minutes. Flip, cooking until golden brown on other side. Adjust heat if necessary to prevent scorching. Fry the remaining patties.
10. Drain on paper towels and serve.

Serves 4

Food

Bulgarians enjoy a hearty traditional cuisine that draws on a wide variety of meats, fruits, and vegetables. Bulgarians begin many meals with thick soups. Monastery soup contains beans and vegetables. Cucumber, walnuts, yogurt, and dill are the ingredients in cold *tarator* soup. Lamb, veal (calf meat), and pork are central to many Bulgarian dishes, including *kebabche* (grilled meat patties spiced with black pepper, onions, and paprika). *Kavarma* is a hot stew containing pork, mushrooms, and vegetables. Other common ingredients in Bulgarian cooking are eggplant, tomatoes, carrots, goat cheese, and potatoes.

Known as *kiselo mlyako*, Bulgarian yogurt is made from the milk of sheep, goats, or cows. *Banitsa*, a sweet, cheese-filled pastry, is often eaten with yogurt for dessert. Bulgarians also enjoy a wide variety of fresh fruits, including cherries, strawberries, apricots, raspberries, apples, pears, melons, plums, and grapes.

Bulgarians drink fruit juices, lemonade, tea, and thick, strong coffee. Adults often have *slivova rakiya* (plum or grape brandy) before meals. Bulgaria also produces red and white wines, as well as a liqueur made from rose petals.

Sports and Recreation

Like many Europeans, Bulgarians love soccer (called football in Europe). All major cities have soccer teams, and young and old Bulgarians follow local teams with great interest. The Bulgarian national team won a bronze medal at the annual World Cup soccer championships in 1994.

Bulgaria has produced many champion weight lifters and wrestlers. At the 2000 Summer Olympics in Sydney, Australia, Armen Nazaryan won a gold medal in Greco-Roman wrestling and Galabin Boevski took home a gold in weight lifting. Weight lifter Milen Dobrev won a gold medal at the 2004 Olympic Games in Athens, Greece. Bulgaria also has star track-and-field athletes, such as the world-record-holding high jumper Stefka Kostadinova and triple jumper Theresa Marinova. Magdalena Maleeva is a longtime fixture on the women's professional tennis tour.

Many Bulgarians participate in recreational sports, such as hiking and mountain climbing. The Black Sea coast offers waterskiing, sailing, and windsurfing. Downhill skiers enjoy the slopes in the Pirin and Rila mountains. Many tourists come to Bulgaria to ski, hike, and take part in other outdoor recreation.

Some Bulgarians like to play backgammon, a board game originally from the Middle East. Others enjoy chess, which originated in India. Bulgarian Antoaneta Stefanova is the third-highest-ranking female chess player in the world.

Gergana Kirilova of Bulgaria attempts to lift **240 pounds (110 kilograms) at the 2003 World Weightlifting Championship in Canada. Kirlova** won all the gold medals in her weight category in the **2004 European championship.**

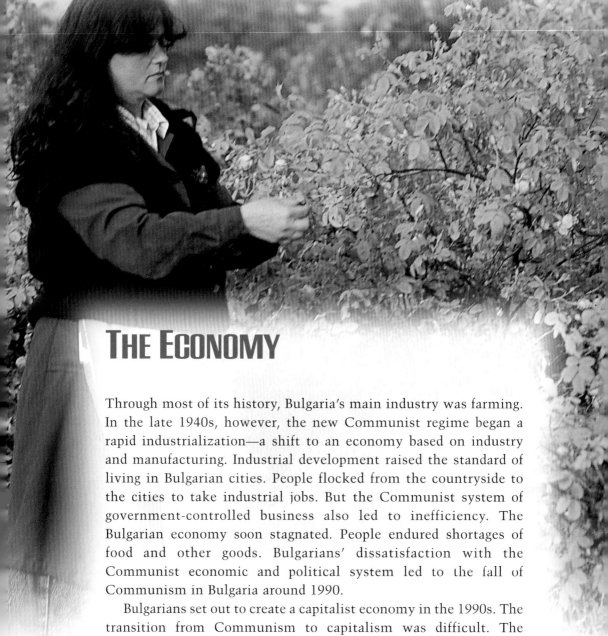

THE ECONOMY

Through most of its history, Bulgaria's main industry was farming. In the late 1940s, however, the new Communist regime began a rapid industrialization—a shift to an economy based on industry and manufacturing. Industrial development raised the standard of living in Bulgarian cities. People flocked from the countryside to the cities to take industrial jobs. But the Communist system of government-controlled business also led to inefficiency. The Bulgarian economy soon stagnated. People endured shortages of food and other goods. Bulgarians' dissatisfaction with the Communist economic and political system led to the fall of Communism in Bulgaria around 1990.

Bulgarians set out to create a capitalist economy in the 1990s. The transition from Communism to capitalism was difficult. The nation's factories, farms, and other businesses had operated inefficiently for many years. Equipment was out of date. Except for other former Soviet-bloc nations, Bulgaria had not developed strong trade

relationships with foreign countries. It also owed large amounts of money—roughly $12 billion—to international lenders. The 1990s were marked by unemployment, corruption in business and government, and inflation.

In the early 2000s, the economic situation has improved somewhat. The government has passed new tax and banking laws, has made trade deals with foreign countries, has raised the minimum wage for workers, and has stemmed inflation. Bulgaria's leaders are working with the International Monetary Fund to bolster the country's economy.

Despite such efforts, the nation's economy still has a long way to go. Roughly 18 percent of Bulgaria's people are unemployed. More than 12 percent live below the poverty line. The typical Bulgarian worker takes home only about $110 per month.

The most promising plan for Bulgaria is its effort to join the European Union (EU), an economic and political association of European nations. Membership in the EU would make it easier for

Drug and weapons traffickers operate in Bulgaria. They move shipments between Europe, Russia, Turkey, and elsewhere. Many "Mafia-style" organized-crime groups are in this business.

Bulgaria to trade and do business with other European nations; would allow Bulgaria to use the Euro, the common European currency; and would offer other economic benefits. If Bulgaria can meet the EU's strict political and economic guidelines, it could enter the association in 2005.

Services

The service sector—businesses such as health care, banking, communications, insurance, and tourism—accounts for approximately 58 percent of Bulgaria's gross domestic product (GDP, the total value of all goods and services produced in the nation in one year).

During the Communist era, very few foreigners were allowed to visit Bulgaria. With the fall of Communism, tourism became one of the nation's most promising service industries. International travelers come to Bulgaria to enjoy the country's beaches, ski areas, cities, and rural villages. The nation has built new hotels and seaside resorts to

Sunny Black Sea beaches attract visitors from Bulgaria and foreign countries. Visit www.vgsbooks.com for links to websites with information about Bulgaria's tourist industry.

attract more vacationers. In 2000 more than two million tourists visited Bulgaria, spending nearly $1 billion. The tourist industry employs about 130,000 Bulgarians.

Industry

Industry, including manufacturing, mining, and power generation, is the second-largest economic sector in Bulgaria. This sector accounts for 29 percent of the GDP.

Bulgarian firms manufacture machinery, chemicals, iron and steel, plastics, fertilizers, and pharmaceutical products. Oil and gas refineries and food and tobacco processing plants also operate in Bulgaria. Each year Bulgaria exports more than $5 billion in goods, including clothing, footwear, iron and steel, machinery, and fuel. Its major export partners are Italy, Germany, Turkey, Greece, France, and the United States.

Miners extract iron ore, copper, zinc, and lead from sites around the nation, along with small amounts of gold, silver, and uranium. Bulgaria has coal reserves around Sofia and in the Maritsa River valley and small stocks of oil and natural gas. Hydroelectric power stations operate on several Bulgarian rivers. A nuclear power plant at the city of Kozloduy, one of the largest nuclear plants in the world, generates much of the country's electricity.

Visit www.vgsbooks.com for links to websites with additional information about tourism, industry, and agriculture in Bulgaria.

Bulgaria has had to retool its industries, such as this **Communist-era factory,** to compete in the modern economy.

Grapes flourish in the **vineyards of central Bulgaria.** Some areas of the region have been producing wine since the sixth century B.C.

Agriculture

Agriculture, including farming, fishing, and forestry, accounts for 14 percent of Bulgaria's GDP. With the end of Communism, large collective farms have been broken apart, and plots of land have been returned to individual farmers. The typical farm is small—less than 3 acres (1.2 hectares)—and is worked by a single family.

Farmers on the Danubian Plain grow mostly grains such as wheat, corn, barley, and rye. On the Thracian Plain, farmers grow a wide variety of vegetables and fruits, as well as cotton, rice, and tobacco. Vineyards near the Black Sea and on the Thracian Plain produce grapes, for making red and white wines. In the Valley of the Roses, in central Bulgaria, farmers grow millions of pink and white roses. The oil from rose petals, or attar, is then used to add the fragrance of roses to expensive perfumes.

Bulgaria has been producing wines since the sixth century B.C. In modern times, Bulgaria is the world's fifth-largest exporter of wine. On February 14, Bulgarians honor Saint Trifon, the patron saint (protector) of vineyards.

Goats have long been prized possessions in Bulgaria. In rural villages in the Rhodope Mountains, people use goat's milk to make yogurt and cheese. They eat salted goat's meat. They weave goat hair into rugs and turn goat skin into sandals and other items.

Other farmers grow herbs, sunflowers, or sugar beets. Many farmers raise livestock, especially goats, whose milk is made into yogurt and cheese. Many Bulgarians make a living by fishing in the Black Sea, pulling anchovies, mullets, mackerels, and other species from the water. The fish is then processed and canned or sold fresh at food markets. Bulgaria's main agricultural exports include herbs, tobacco, wine, and attar of roses.

Bulgaria's Valley of the Roses produces about 70 percent of the world's attar of roses, the oil for making perfume. It takes about 250 pounds (113 kg) of rose petals to make a single ounce of attar, a substance worth more than gold on world markets.

 Visit www.vgsbooks.com for links to websites with additional information about the Valley of the Roses.

Both cars and buses provide **transportation in Plovdiv, Bulgaria.**

Transportation

Bulgarian towns and cities are linked by a large network of roads and railroads. The nation has more than 23,000 miles (40,233 km) of roads. Most roads in Bulgaria (94 percent) are paved, but many are bumpy and full of potholes. In rural areas, farm animals and horse-drawn carts often share the roads with cars.

Many Bulgarians can't afford cars but instead travel by public transportation, including buses, trams, and trains. Travelers can use the Bulgarian State Railways to travel from city to city, although trains can be slow or infrequent, and delays are common. Buses also travel between cities. In most Bulgarian cities, buses and trams carry travelers where they need to go.

The nation has 128 airports with paved runways, with an international airport in Sofia. At Black Sea ports such as Burgas, Nesebâr, and Varna, cargo ships and tankers bring goods from other nations to Bulgaria and vice versa. Commercial ships also travel along the Danube River. Railcars carry goods to and from other nations, as well as between Bulgarian cities.

The Future

If positive trends continue, Bulgaria's future will be bright. The transition to capitalism, although difficult at first, is starting to pay off in new businesses and a stable economy. Bulgaria's ski resorts are booming, Bulgarian banks are growing stronger, and agricultural exports have increased. Experts feel that the economy is right on track for upcoming EU membership.

Bulgaria's people—especially the young—are excited to be living in a free and democratic society. The outpouring of new literature, music, and art in the twenty-first century is a testament to the nation's vitality and optimism. Bulgarians have overcome many hardships in their long and rich history. They are survivors. Whatever challenges the future holds, Bulgarians are sure to approach them with strength, creativity, and hope.

Timeline

ca. 40,000 B.C. Stone Age cave dwellers live in Bulgaria.

ca. 5000 Ancient Bulgarians begin to build permanent villages.

ca. 1000 The Thracian civilization develops in Bulgaria.

600s Greek settlers arrive in Thrace.

346 Philip of Macedonia defeats the Thracians.

A.D. 46 The Romans establish control over the Balkan Peninsula.

395 Bulgaria becomes part of the Byzantine Empire.

400s Slavs from the north move into Bulgaria.

600s Bulgars from Central Asia arrive in Bulgaria.

681 Khan Asparukh establishes the First Bulgarian Empire.

863 Khan Boris I establishes Christianity as Bulgaria's official religion.

893–927 Czar Simeon expands the Bulgarian Empire throughout most of the Balkans.

CA. 900 Bulgarians adopt the Cyrillic alphabet.

1014 Under Emperor Basil II, the Byzantines conquer Bulgaria.

1180s Brothers Petâr and Asen lead a rebellion against the Byzantines and establish the Second Bulgarian Empire. Veliko Turnovo becomes the empire's capital.

1360s The Ottoman Turks invade the Balkan Peninsula.

1396 The Ottomans annex Bulgaria to their empire.

1762 Paisii Hilendarski publishes *The Slav-Bulgarian History*, beginning the National Revival period.

1876 The Bulgarians revolt unsuccessfully against Ottoman rule.

1877 Russia declares war on and defeats the Ottoman Empire.

1878 Bulgaria becomes a principality but remains partially under Ottoman control.

1879 Sofia becomes the capital of Bulgaria. Bulgaria creates a constitution.

1908 Bulgaria declares its complete independence from the Ottoman Empire.

1912–1913 Bulgaria, Serbia, and Greece fight the Turks in the First Balkan War.

1913 Bulgaria fights Serbia, Greece, and Turkey in the Second Balkan War.

1915–1918 Bulgaria joins the Central Powers to fight during World War I.

1941 Bulgaria joins the Axis in World War II.

1943 Allied planes drop bombs on Sofia and other Bulgarian cities, causing widespread destruction.

1944 Soviet forces occupy Bulgaria.

1946 Communists create a new government and new constitution in Bulgaria.

1962 Todor Zhivkov becomes the Bulgarian head of state.

1988 The Bulgarian State Female Vocal Choir wins its first Grammy award for best traditional folk recording.

1989 Citizens protest against Communist rule in Bulgaria and other Eastern European nations.

1990 Bulgaria holds multiparty elections and begins the transition to a free-market, democratic society.

1996 Bulgaria undergoes a severe economic downturn.

2001 Simeon II, Bulgaria's former king, becomes the nation's prime minister.

2003 Bulgaria joins a U.S.-led coalition to invade Iraq.

2004 Bulgaria joins the North Atlantic Treaty Organization (NATO).

COUNTRY NAME Republic of Bulgaria

AREA 42,823 square miles (110,911 sq. km)

MAIN LANDFORMS Danubian Plain, Balkan Mountains, Sredna Gora, Thracian Plain, Burgas Lowland, Rhodope Mountains

HIGHEST POINT Musala Peak (9,597 feet; 2,925 m)

LOWEST POINT Sea level

MAJOR RIVERS Danube, Iskur, Kamchiya, Maritsa, Mesta, Struma,

ANIMALS boars, carp, deer, elks, foxes, owls, pelicans, quails, sturgeon, turtledoves, whitefish, wildcats, wolves

CAPITAL CITY Sofia

OTHER MAJOR CITIES Plovdiv, Varna, Burgas

OFFICIAL LANGUAGE Bulgarian

MONETARY UNIT lev; 100 stotinki = 1 lev

BULGARIAN CURRENCY

The Bulgarian unit of currency is called the lev, which is divided into 100 stotinki. Bulgarian money comes in 1-, 2-, 5-, 10-, 20-, and 50-lev paper notes and 1-, 2-, 5-, 10-, 20-, and 50-stotinki coins. In 2004, 1 lev equaled about 62 cents in U.S. money.

In 1999 Bulgaria issued new currency because its old money had lost most of its value due to inflation. The new currency shows portraits of some of Bulgaria's most famous historical and cultural figures, including Saint John of Rila, a ninth-century Bulgarian holy man; Father Paisii Hilendarski, the monk who spearheaded the National Revival; and Ivan Milov, an early twentieth-century painter.

Bulgaria's flag consists of three horizontal stripes: white on top, green in the middle, and red on the bottom. White stands for freedom and peace. Green stands for Bulgaria's farms and forests. Red stands for blood shed in the struggle for independence. Bulgarians adopted the flag in 1879, upon winning partial independence from Turkey. In 1947 Bulgaria's Communist-era coat of arms was added to the flag. The coat of arms was dropped shortly after Communism fell.

Bulgaria's national anthem, "Mila Rodino" (My Homeland), was written by Tsvetan Tsvetkov Radoslavov, a student and soldier. Radoslavov wrote the song in 1885, but it did not become the national anthem until 1964. Here is an English translation of the first verse and chorus:

Proudly rise the Balkan peaks,
At their feet Blue Danube flows;
Over Thrace the sun is shining,
Pirin looms in purple glow.

CHORUS
Oh, dear native land,
Earthly paradise!
For your loveliness, your beauty
E'er will charm our eyes.

 Go to www.vgsbooks.com for a link that will let you listen to the national anthem, "Mila Rodino."

Flag National Anthem

VALYA BALKANSKA (b. 1942) Born in Smolyan, Balkanska is considered one of Bulgaria's greatest living treasures. A folk singer, she specializes in the music of the Rhodope Mountains. She sings at folk festivals and concerts in Bulgaria and other nations, frequently accompanied by bagpiper Petâr Yanev. In 1977 the National Aeronautics and Space Administration (NASA) created a laser disc recording of earth sounds, including music and animal calls, and placed it on the *Voyager I* and *Voyager II* spacecraft. The recording was meant to be an introduction to earth in case the craft encountered intelligent life. The record included Balkanska's performance of a Bulgarian folk song.

CHRISTO (b. 1935) The world-famous sculptor Christo was born Christo Javacheff in the Bulgarian city of Gabrovo. As a young man, he attended the Fine Arts Academy in Sofia. He also studied in Vienna, Austria, then moved to Paris, France, and then New York City. Christo began his career making small sculptures out of cans, bottles, paper, plastic, and fabric. In the late 1960s, he began to make giant outdoor projects, wrapping entire buildings and bridges in vast sheets of plastic or fabric. In 1983 he encircled eleven islands off the Florida coast with 6 million square feet (557,400 sq. m) of floating pink polypropylene. In 2005 Christo is scheduled to complete a project called *The Gates,* a series of 7,500 saffron-colored cloth gates that will snake along 23 miles (37 km) of walkways in Central Park in New York. Christo often works in collaboration with his wife, Jeanne-Claude.

NICOLAI GHIAUROV (1929–2004) Ghiaurov was a world-famous opera singer born in Velingrad. As a young man, he studied at the Sofia Musical Academy and later in Moscow in the Soviet Union. He debuted with the Sofia National Opera in 1955. A bass (male singer with the lowest vocal range) who specialized in late nineteenth-century works, he performed with nearly every major world opera, including the Metropolitan Opera in New York City. Ghiaurov often performed with his wife, Italian soprano Mirella Freni. For much of his career, he made his home in Italy.

GEORGI IVANOV (b. 1940) Ivanov was the first Bulgarian cosmonaut—an astronaut with the Soviet space program. Born in the Bulgarian city of Lovech, he trained as a pilot and engineer. In 1979 he and Russian-born cosmonaut Nikolay Rukavishnikov flew into space aboard *Soyuz 33* on a mission to rendezvous (meet up) with the *Salyut 6* Soviet space station. Encountering technical problems, Ivanov and Rukavishnikov were not able to complete the mission. They returned to Earth after almost two days in orbit. After retiring from the space program, Ivanov became a partner in Air Sofia airlines. He is also chairman of the Bulgarian Golf Federation.

STEFKA KOSTADINOVA (b. 1965) High jumper Kostadinova was born in Plovdiv. As a teenager, she attended the Plovdiv School of Sports, first focusing on gymnastics and swimming and then switching to track and field. In 1984, at the age of nineteen, Kostadinova set the women's high jump record in Paris with a jump of 2.05 meters. In 1987 she broke her own mark with a jump of 2.09 meters. The record still stands. Kostadinova won a silver medal at the 1988 Summer Olympics in Seoul, South Korea. She won a gold at the Summer Games in Atlanta in 1996. She has been named Sportsman of the Year of Bulgaria four times and has also served as vice president of the Bulgarian Athletic Federation.

GEORGI MARKOV (1929–1978) Born in Sofia, Markov was a great novelist and playwright. His early novels include *Men, Portrait of My Double,* and *The Women of Warsaw.* In 1969 he staged a play, *The Man Who Was Me,* that angered Bulgarian Communist officials. Fearing for his life, Markov fled to London, England. There, he went to work for a number of broadcast organizations, including the British Broadcasting Corporation and Radio Free Europe. From London Markov spoke out loudly against Bulgaria's Communist government, using both literary works and radio to carry his message. The Bulgarian government labeled Markov a traitor and tried to kill him. The first two attempts failed, but in 1978 a Bulgarian agent managed to stab Markov with a poison-tipped umbrella below the Waterloo Bridge in London. He died three days later.

SIMEON II (b. 1937) Simeon Saxe-Coburg-Gotha was born in Sofia, the son of King Boris III. At the age of six, he became king when his father died. Because he was still a child, his uncle, Prince Kyril, governed in his place. When Soviet-backed Communists took power in Bulgaria in 1944, they assassinated Prince Kyril and many of his staff. Simeon was allowed to stay on the throne, but two years later, the Bulgarian monarchy was abolished. Simeon and the rest of his family fled to Egypt and later Madrid, Spain. Simeon remained in Spain, studying law and business. He also studied at a junior college in the United States. He lived primarily in Spain throughout the Communist era but always kept his ties to Bulgaria. Finally, in 2001, he returned to run for (and win) the office of prime minister.

ANTOANETA STEFANOVA (b. 1979) Stefanova, born in Sofia, is a master chess player. She stands at number three in the world on the World Chess Federation's ranking of female players. Stefanova learned to play chess when she was just four years old. Her first teacher was her father, and her first opponent was her big sister. At the age of ten, in 1989, Stefanova won a children's world championship in Puerto Rico. By the age of thirteen, she was entering adult competitions. Stefanova holds the World Chess Federation ranking of grand master, a title held by only seven women in the world.

ALEXSANDAR NEVSKI CHURCH This grand church in Sofia was built to honor the 200,000 Russians who were killed or wounded fighting the Turks in 1877–1878, especially those who defended Shipka Pass. Built between 1892 and 1912, the building features gold-covered domes, elaborate frescoes, and soaring columns. The church has a large collection of icons, some dating from medieval times.

BURGAS LAKES The four lakes near the city of Burgas are home to 60 percent of Bulgaria's bird species. The lakes also serve as a stopping-off point for birds that migrate each year from Scandinavia (where they summer) to Africa (where they winter) and back again. The winged travelers include storks, pelicans, cranes, buzzards, eagles, and hawks. Bird-watchers flock here each spring and fall to view the birds as they pass through. The lakes area contains nature trails, a conservation center, and other attractions for visitors.

KÂRDZHALI ROCK FORMATIONS With names such as Stone Wedding, Rock Window, and Broken Mountain, the rock formations near the town of Kârdzhali are spectacular to see. The odd-shaped, multicolored formations were created by erupting volcanoes 40 million years ago. Among the fascinating sites are the Rocks at Ustra, giant purple stones in the shape of prisms, cones, and stairways.

RILA MONASTERY Bulgaria's largest and most famous monastery, Rila Monastery occupies a peaceful valley in the Rila Mountains. The monastery was founded in 927 by Ivan Rilski (also known as Saint John of Rila), leader of a colony of monks. Visitors to the monastery will see its splendid church, courtyards, and religious artwork and objects, along with spectacular views of the Rila Mountains. The monastery was named a UNESCO World Heritage Site in 1983. Every year thousands of pilgrims (religious travelers) visit the monastery to take part in worship services.

TSAREVETS FORTRESS The fortress is in Veliko Turnovo, the former capital of Bulgaria. The Byzantines built the original complex between the fifth and seventh centuries A.D. It was rebuilt and expanded over the centuries by Slavs, Bulgars, and again the Byzantines. Turkish invaders destroyed the fortress in 1393. Much of the site has been excavated. Visitors can see remains of the fortress walls, watchtower, monastery, churches, dwellings, palace, and other structures.

VARNA ARCHAEOLOGICAL MUSEUM This museum in the city of Varna houses 100,000 artifacts of Bulgarian history, dating from the Stone Age to the late Middle Ages. Visitors can see six-thousand-year-old gold and copper jewelry, Roman-era plaques and household items, medieval weapons, and much more.

capitalism: an economic system featuring private ownership of business and property, business competition, and little government involvement in business operations

collective farm: a large farm created from a collection of smaller farms and then run by the government

Communism: an economic system featuring government control of business and the economy, government rather than private ownership of property, and an equal distribution of goods and services to all citizens

democracy: a government run by the people. In most democracies, citizens control the government by voting for lawmakers and other government officials.

dictator: a ruler who holds complete authority over a government and nation

Eastern Orthodox Church: a federation of Christian churches in Greece, Russia, Eastern Europe, and western Asia. Some Eastern Orthodox practices and teachings differ from those of the Roman Catholic and Protestant churches, which are also Christian.

free-market economy: an economy in which companies and individuals are free to compete for customers and business, with little government interference

guerrillas: small groups of fighters, not connected to a regular military force, who carry out ambushes, bombings, and raids behind enemy lines

icon: a sacred painting common in the Eastern Orthodox Church. Icons usually depict images of Jesus or a saint.

industrialization: the shift from an economy based on farming to one based on manufacturing

Islam: a major religion in the Middle East, North Africa, and parts of Asia and Europe. People who practice Islam are called Muslims. The Islamic religion was founded on the Arabian Peninsula in the 600s A.D. by the prophet Muhammad. Islam's holy book is the Quran.

monarchy: a government headed by a leader such as a king, queen, or prince, with titles passed down in the family through the generations. Some monarchs hold complete power, while others share their power with other government officials.

monastery: a house for people who have taken religious vows to devote their lives to God and religious work

urbanization: the change from a rural (farm-based) society to one in which people live mostly in big cities

Glossary

BNN: Bulgarian News Network. **2005.**
http://www.bgnewsnet.com
This online newspaper provides up-to-date news articles from Bulgaria as well as international news.

Bousfield, Jonathan, and Dan Richardson. *Bulgaria.* **London: Rough Guides, 2002.**
This comprehensive guidebook provides an overview of Bulgaria for travelers, with sections on history, sightseeing, culture, and language.

The Bulgarian News Agency (BTA). **2005.**
http://www.bta.bg/site/en/indexe.shtml
This website was created by The Bulgarian News Agency, which is Bulgaria's national news carrier. It provides up-to-date news articles from Bulgaria.

Crampton, R. J. A Consice History of Bulgaria. New York: Cambridge University Press, 1997,
The author of this book explores Bulgaria's history and introduces readers to Bulgaria's rich yet conflict-filled past.

Curtis, Glenn E., ed. *Bulgaria: A Country Study.* **Washington, DC: Federal Research Division, Library of Congress, 1993.**
Produced by the Library of Congress, this thorough text examines Bulgarian history from prehistoric times through the Communist era. It includes sections on Bulgaria's natural environment, society, economy, and government.

Embassy of Bulgaria, Washington D.C. **2005.**
http://www.bulgaria-embassy.org/
This website was created by the Bulgarian Embassy located in the United States. It provides information and assistance to those interested in traveling to and from Bulgaria. The site also includes news articles and current information on economic opportunities, as well as an extensive list of links to other informative websites.

Glenny, Misha. *The Balkans: Nationalism, War and the Great Powers, 1804–1999.* **New York: Viking, 2000.**
This detailed book explores Balkan history in the nineteenth and twentieth centuries. It provides extensive coverage of Bulgaria, especially its relationships with other Balkan states.

Greenway, Paul. *Bulgaria.* **Melbourne, AUS: Lonely Planet, 2002.**
Written for tourists, this thorough guidebook offers a detailed overview of Bulgarian history, society, and culture, as well as specifics on shopping, dining, special events, and attractions.

Mazower, Mark. *The Balkans: A Short History.* **New York: The Modern Library, 2000.**
The author looks at the history of the Balkan Peninsula, from Slavic settlement in the sixth century A.D. to the present day. Bulgaria's history is woven into the story of the peninsula as a whole.

Selected Bibliography

Thompson, Wayne C. *Nordic, Central, and Southeastern Europe 2002.* **Harpers Ferry, WV: Stryker-Post, 2002.**
This annual publication offers a comprehensive look at the nations of central Europe, from Scandinavia south to the Balkans. A chapter on Bulgaria is included, with detailed discussions of the nation's history, economy, government, and culture.

The World Factbook: Bulgaria. **2004.**
http://www.cia.gov/publications/factbook/geos/bu.html
This site, written by the Central Intelligence Agency, offers facts and statistics on present-day Bulgaria. It includes information on government, the economy, health, communications, and other areas of Bulgarian life.

Bulgaria.com
http://www.bulgaria.com

This informative site provides extensive information on Bulgaria's history, with additional material on famous Bulgarians, the government, and travel in Bulgaria. Visitors can also find sources for Bulgarian music and books about Bulgaria.

Country Profile: Bulgaria, 2004
http://news.bbc.co.uk/1/hi/world/europe/ country_profiles/1059735.stm

Created by the British Broadcasting Corporation, this site provides a quick overview of Bulgarian leaders, statistics, media, and history. Visitors will also find links to Bulgarian government and language sites.

Harvey, Miles. *The Fall of the Soviet Union*. Chicago: Children's Press, 1995.

In this book for young readers, the author looks at the powerful Soviet Union, including its history, then examines the nation's breakup into independent republics in 1991. Vivid photos add insight into the text.

Kort, Michael. *The Handbook of the New Eastern Europe*. Brookfield, CT: Twenty-First Century Books, 2001.

The author explores Eastern Europe after the fall of Communism, with country-by-country profiles. Readers will learn about the challenges facing Bulgaria and other nations as they try to create democratic governments and free-market economies.

Popescu, Julian. *Bulgaria*. Philadelphia: Chelsea House, 2000.

This book for young readers provides a solid overview of Bulgarian history, culture, government, and society. Maps and illustrations accompany the text.

Roberts, J. M. *Eastern Asia and Classical Greece*. New York: Oxford University Press, 2001.

This richly illustrated book for young readers examines Greece and the ancient world, including the Thracian civilization that thrived in Bulgaria in ancient times. Maps and sidebars accompany the text.

Ruggiero, Adriane. *The Ottoman Empire*. New York: Benchmark Books, 2002.

The Ottoman Turks once ruled a vast empire, including Bulgaria and the Balkans. This book looks at the empire using detailed text, maps, and artwork.

Schönfeldt, Sybil Grafin, and Iassen Ghiuselev. *Orpheus and Eurydia*. Los Angeles: J. Paul Getty Trust, 2001.

Using beautiful illustrations, this book tells the story of the musician Orpheus and his love for the wood nymph Eurydice. According to Greek mythology, Orpheus was born in the kingdom of Thrace, the forerunner of modern-day Bulgaria.

Further Reading and Websites

Sofia News Agency
http://www.novinite.com
This news site offers up-to-date information from Bulgaria, with stories on business, politics, and sports. The site includes links to other Bulgarian groups, including radio stations, businesses, and arts organizations.

vgsbooks.com
http://www.vgsbooks.com
Visit vgsbooks.com, the homepage of the Visual Geography Series®. You can get linked to all sorts of useful on-line information, including geographical, historical, demographic, cultural, and economic websites. The vgsbooks.com site is a great resource for late-breaking news and statistics.

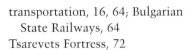
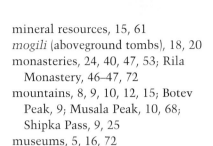

mineral resources, 15, 61
mogili (aboveground tombs), 18, 20
monasteries, 24, 40, 47, 53; Rila
    Monastery, 46–47, 72
mountains, 8, 9, 10, 12, 15; Botev
    Peak, 9; Musala Peak, 10, 68;
    Shipka Pass, 9, 25
museums, 5, 16, 72
music, 5, 49–50, 65
musical instruments, 49

national anthem, 69
national parks, 14
natural resources, 15
North Atlantic Treaty Organization
    (NATO), 36, 67

Petkova, Bora Nikolaeva, 49
Plovdiv, 16, 20, 64, 68
pollution. *See* environmental issues
population, 4, 16, 39, 40

Rachev, Rumen, 48
Rakovski, Georgi, 24, 25
recipe (feta cheese and potato
    patties), 56
religion, 52–54. *See also* monasteries
reserves, wildlife, 14
rivers, 9, 10, 12, 13, 15, 61, 68; Arda,
    10; Danube, 8, 10, 12, 14, 64, 68;
    Maritsa, 12, 16, 68

services, 60–61
Simeon II, 29, 30, 34, 67, 71
Sofia, 9, 10, 15, 16, 31, 38;
    Aleksandâr Nevski Church, 32, 72;
    became capital, 16, 26, 66, 68;
    climate, 12; coal reserves, 61;
    health care, 41; National Opera
    House, 16, 49, 70; population, 16;
    Sofia City Garden, 16; Sofia
    Musical Academy, 70;
    transportation, 16, 36, 64, 70;
    University of Sofia, 42; World War
    II bombing, 16, 30, 67
Soviet bloc, 5, 30, 58
Spassov, Teodossi, 50
sports and recreation, 57

tourism, 5, 17, 57, 60–61

transportation, 16, 64; Bulgarian
    State Railways, 64
Tsarevets Fortress, 72

United States: trade with Bulgaria,
    61; war on terrorism, 34, 36, 67

Valley of the Roses, 9, 44, 56–57, 62,
    63
Varna, 12, 13, 15, 16–17, 64, 68

women, 39, 44–45. *See also*
    Balkanska, Valya; Bulgarian State
    Female Vocal Choir; Dimitrova,
    Blaga; Petkova, Bora Nikolaeva
words, Bulgarian. *See* language
World War I, 27–28
World War II, 5, 16, 29–30, 38, 48

Zograf, Zahari, 47

Captions for photos appearing on cover and chapter openers:

Cover: A bridge crosses the Yantra River in the town of Veliko Turnovo. Thousands of tourists visit this historical site, which served as Bulgaria's capital city from 1186 to 1394.

pp. 4–5 Folk dancers in traditional costume perform in Sofia, the Bulgarian capital.

pp. 8–9 The Balkan Mountains are a prominent feature of central Bulgaria. The Bulgarian name for the Balkan Mountains is Stara Planina—"old mountains" in Bulgarian. The name Balkan comes from the Turkish word for mountain.

pp. 18–19 This roof mural painted on a Thracian tomb in Kazanlâk dates from the fourth-century B.C.

pp. 38–39 A group of students takes a field trip in Plovdiv.

pp. 46–47 Ceiling frescoes (paintings on plaster) in the Rila Monastery are nineteenth-century re-creations of much older works that were lost in a fire in the 1830s.

pp. 58–59 Bulgarian women harvest roses in their nation's famous Valley of the Roses.

Photo Acknowledgments

The images in this book are used with the permission of: © Kurt Scholz/ SuperStock, pp. 4–5, 55; © Digital Cartographics, pp. 6, 11; © Martin Barlow/ Art Directors, pp. 8–9, 15, 31, 38–39, 52, 60, 61, 62, 64; © Jean Hall/Art Directors, pp. 10, 14, 63; © STOYAN NENOV/Reuters/CORBIS, pp. 13, 35; © Jim Love/Art Directors, pp. 17, 44; © Ivor Wellbelove/Art Directors, pp. 18–19, 32, 58–59; Gordon Rose, p. 20; Susan and Randall Baker, p. 23; © Independent Picture Service/*A Short History of Bulgaria*, pp. 24, 25; Library of Congress, p. 27 (LC-B2-904-2), 29 top (LC-B2-1020-13); United States Holocaust Memorial Museum (courtesy of Estelle Bechoefer), p. 29 (bottom); © Chris Niedenthal/Time Life Pictures/Getty Images, p. 33; © Reuters/ CORBIS, p. 34; © DIMITAR DILKOFF/AFP/Getty Images, pp. 36, 41; Land O' Lakes International Development, pp. 37, 54; © Ed Kashi/CORBIS, p. 43; © B. Woods/Art Directors, pp. 46–47; © Tom Lawson/BIPs/Getty Images, p. 48; Elektra Nonesuch, p. 49; © José F. Poblete/CORBIS, p. 50; © LYLE STAFFORD/Reuters/CORBIS, p. 57; www.banknotes.com, p. 68.

Cover photo: © Sandro Vannini/CORBIS. Back cover: NASA.

JAN